Diet Simply...
With Soup

Diet Simply... With Soup

Gail L. Becker, R.D.

Foreword by Dr. Antonio M. Gotto

PUBLISHED BY POCKET BOOKS NEW YORK

Another *Original* publication of POCKET BOOKS

POCKET BOOKS, a division of Simon & Schuster, Inc.
1230 Avenue of the Americas, New York, N.Y. 10020

ISBN: 0-671-46428-0

First Pocket Books printing October, 1983

10 9 8 7 6 5 4 3 2 1

Contents

I would like to acknowledge Dr. Antonio Gotto, Dr. John P. Foreyt and Ms. Becky Reeves, R.D., all from Baylor College of Medicine for their invaluable contribution in the preparation of this book.

A special thanks to Kim Stambaugh who motivated me to be more personally aware of opportunities for adding time for exercise in my own life.

I would also like to thank Marsha Hudnall, R.D., and Trisha Gorman for their endless hours of dedication in helping me put it all together.

Foreword

As our population becomes more and more health conscious and the individual assumes a greater responsibility for the maintenance of good health and prevention of disease, diet is gaining increased recognition for the part it plays in attaining these goals. And as a principle of a healthy life-style—along with physical fitness, avoidance of tobacco, non-essential drugs and excess alcohol, and a balance between play and work—a proper diet based on a variety of foods is a recommendation that most physicians endorse.

Today many Americans need to reduce their calorie intake in order to reach their goal of a healthy diet. But with the variety of weight-control diets available today, many people are overwhelmed and confused. Fad diets are numerous, and although they may result in a substantial weight reduction over a short period of time, that reduction is usually not long maintained. The reason for this is that unless a diet can be adapted to a long-term period of maintenance, it is likely to be soon discarded. The pounds that have been rapidly lost are rapidly regained. This is the history of most chronic dieters.

Diet Simply . . . With Soup represents an interesting approach to weight reduction and control by incorporating soup and good eating habits into a plan to significantly decrease caloric intake over a long period of time. Most nutritionists and physicians who counsel patients and the general public about diet agree that eating slowly is an effective behavior modification technique for weight control. Featuring the technique of eating soup slowly under specified conditions, *Diet Simply . . . With Soup* introduces a dietary approach that combines the latest information on nutrition with this and other behavior modification techniques to present three well-balanced diets which can help the dieter reach his or her weight goal.

ANTONIO M. GOTTO, JR., M.D.
Chairman, Department of Internal Medicine
Baylor College of Medicine
The Methodist Hospital

I

Not Just Another Diet Book

This is not an ordinary diet book, though it contains dieting and menu suggestions. It isn't a simple exercise book, either, though an entire chapter is devoted to the importance of an active life-style.

This is a book about change. It's about changing your eating and exercise habits and, most importantly, your attitudes towards them.

Dieters often become fixated on one aspect of weight control. Some focus all their efforts on counting calories, without moving a muscle. They don't realize that by losing weight without exercising, they end up looking thinner, but flabby. Others take up jogging with a passion, and then use it as an excuse to eat all the pecan pie their hearts desire. Overweight people who exercise without dieting may be dismayed to learn that they end up powerful, but stocky—not with the svelte look they envisioned.

What most dieters don't realize is that weight loss is like a three-legged stool. One leg is a nutritious food plan that reduces caloric intake. It is balanced against the second leg: an exercise plan in which more calories are expended than are taken in under the food plan. The third leg is what keeps the stool from toppling over. It is a behavior modification program to teach new habits and insure that the weight loss is maintained over time.

Are you a "diet diehard"—someone thoroughly committed to dieting as the only path to weight loss? Perhaps you're sensitive to the way you look when exercising. Yet, isn't the main impetus for losing weight the fact that you feel unattractive simply standing still?[1] You might do well to remember that 95 percent of people who diet without exercising gain that weight right back.[2]

Some people are discouraged from exercising by the fact that losing inches through exercise (alone) is a relatively slow process when compared to dieting (alone).[1] However, research shows that the longer it takes to lose weight, the longer the weight will stay off.[3] What we're aiming for here is long-term weight loss, not instant but short-lived success.

As you read on, you will learn many strategies to help change the habits that led to your current weight problems. One of these strategies is the inspiration for this book. It is the discovery that by eating slowly, we consume fewer calories. The reason for this is that it takes 20 minutes for the body to tell the brain that it is full.[4]

There are several ways to help you slow down at mealtime. One is to make a lot of conversation. Another is to chew each mouthful 10 times, and lay down your utensils between each bite. A fourth idea is to take "time out" for a few minutes about one-third of the way through the meal.

One strategy to slow down food consumption is to eat hot soup at the start of a meal. Not only have diets that include soup been connected with weight loss, soup also makes good nutritional sense. A University of Pennsylvania study of 1000 people who were at least 15 pounds overweight found that those who ate soup with meals consumed almost 60 calories per meal less than those who didn't.[5] Moreover, the average intake of calories for the entire day was reduced by 92 calories when soup was eaten at lunch.

Dieters who had soup four or more times a week shed an average of 20 percent of their excess weight over the 10-week test period, compared to those who had soup less than four times a week—who lost 15 percent of their excess weight on the diet program.

The researchers found that meals in which soup was included tended to be eaten more slowly than nonsoup meals. For example, in comparing lunches in which either yogurt or soup was served, soup lunches were eaten at a rate of 15.9 calories per minute, while yogurt lunches were consumed at a pace of 22.1 calories per minute.

Experts from leading universities examined the relationship between food consumption and health by using data from two large U.S. government studies (The Ten State Nutrition Survey [1968-1970] and the Health and Nutrition Examination Survey [1971-1974]). They discovered that people who had certain patterns of food consumption had less clinical symptoms of nutritional deficiency than others. People who showed the fewest signs or symptoms of nutrition-related problems were those who consumed an average amount of all foods but ate more soup and dairy products, and ate the least amount of sugary foods and drinks.[6] This was true regardless of socioeconomic standing, region of the country or age. Those who ate fewer dairy products and more sugary beverages showed the most symptoms of nutrition-related problems.

Dr. Arnold E. Schaefer, one of the investigators of this study, cautions that too many factors influence health (such as heredity, environment and life-style) for anyone to claim that food alone determines health. However, he says that analysis serves to emphasize that types of food consumed do play a role. Referring to the nourishing qualities of soup, Dr. Schaefer says, "Sometimes it takes a scientific effort to prove a principle that our grandmothers knew instinctively."

In the next chapter, Dr. John Foreyt, a psychologist who specializes in behavior modification, will help you become psychologically better prepared for dieting. He will provide a step-by-step plan to help you break eating habits you may not have even been aware of.

In Chapter III, exercise instructor Kim Stambaugh explains the importance of a regular exercise program while you diet. The developer of a style of stretching movements known as Kinetics, Kim offers easy exercise you can do at home or at work any time of the day. The chapter closes with exercises specifically designed to reduce six problem spots, such as thighs, arms or neck. Each exercise includes one version for beginners, one for advanced exercisers.

The succeeding chapters provide you with three Soup Diet eating plans: the ten-day Kick-Off Diet to get you started on your weight-loss program, the longer-term Take-It-Off Plan for those who need to lose more weight, and the Keep-It-Off-Forever Plan for maintaining your weight loss. Sample menu plans and recipes in the latter half of the book prove that dieting doesn't have to be boring. The recipes have been designed to offer the greatest amount of nutrition with the fewest calories.

II

Getting Ready to Diet

by JOHN FOREYT, Ph.D.

Babies rarely are born overweight. If people become fat as they grow into adolescence or adulthood, it is primarily because of habits picked up along the way. Habits like snacking while watching television or taking elevators when stairs are available. Cleaning your plate at dinner even though you're full, or riding in a golf cart instead of walking. These habits in themselves aren't inherently "bad," but when combined they result in weight gain and all its attendant problems.

The good news about most habits is that they are learned and can be unlearned. The bad news—or so many obese people seem to feel—is that no one can change your habits or lose weight for you. Not friends or family, magazine articles or your psychologist—not even this book. You and you alone are responsible for being overweight, and when you become thin, it will be due to your own efforts, and yours alone.

It wasn't until the late 1960s that doctors began to realize why so many diet and exercise weight-loss programs failed: People approached dieting as a temporary inconvenience to ease guilt, a way to prove to themselves and others that they were "trying to do something about being fat." Even today, some dieters will cut out fudge sundaes with the expectation of digging in again "once the diet is over."

Doctors now know that the way to take weight off and, most importantly, keep it off in the long run, is to make basic life-style changes. We teach patients how to do this through a process called behavior modification. This means changing the eating and exercise behavior patterns that underlie eating and exercise habits.

At our Diet Modification Clinic at the Baylor College of

Medicine in Houston, Texas, we have devised a plan to teach patients how to take control of their eating habits.[7] After two months of behavior modification sessions aimed at changing eating behavior, about three-quarters of the overweight patients were able to maintain their weight loss or continue to lose. So far, our studies have followed these patients only up to a year, but a recent 5-year investigation still being analyzed appears to show the same results.

If you would like to try this plan, follow the suggestions described below. Add a new suggestion one week at a time, while continuing to practice those from the previous weeks. You will get a new suggestion each week for nine weeks. If you repeatedly practice them, many will become habits that will stay with you.

Now, here's the good part. If you satisfactorily follow the suggestion for the week, you get to reward yourself at the end of that week. No, the reward is not your favorite food!

On the following "Pleasure Chart" put an X in the column that indicates how much pleasure each item gives you. When you've finished evaluating, enter into a small notebook the items that you enjoy "very much." These are your rewards—and they may be anything from buying new clothes, to playing golf, to telephoning a faraway friend. Some people find a simple reward in lounging in a bubble bath or taking the phone off the hook, putting on a good record and lying back for an hour doing absolutely nothing! It doesn't have to be complicated, just somewhat special.

If you do not follow a week's suggestion, you must not permit yourself to get your reward. If your reward was "watching my favorite TV show" but you fail to do your assignment, you must walk out of the room even if your whole family is enjoying the program. You can't have it both ways!

If you follow the rules, you will very likely have success. These techniques work!

The Soup Diet Pleasure Chart*

This chart will help you identify various things that give you pleasure. Please check the column that best describes the amount of pleasure each item listed gives you. Omit the items that do not apply to you. At the end of the questionnaire, add any other items that give you pleasure.

	None	A Little	Much	Very Much
1. Watching Television				
2. Listening to the Radio				
3. Listening to the Stereo				
4. Playing Cards and Other Games				
5. Doing Crossword Puzzles				
6. Reading Books or Magazines				
7. Dancing				
8. Sleeping Late				
9. Shopping				
10. Buying New Clothes				
11. Buying Kitchen Appliances				
12. Buying Records				
13. Telephoning a Friend Long Distance				
14. Visiting Friends				
15. Taking a Relaxing Bath				
16. Attending Plays or Concerts				
17. Attending Movies				

*Adapted from form developed by the Diet Modification Clinic, Baylor College of Medicine and The Methodist Hospital.

	None	A Little	Much	Very Much
18. Attending Sporting Events (football, baseball, basketball, hockey, etc.)				
19. Golfing				
20. Bowling				
21. Bicycling				
22. Playing Tennis				
23. Participating in Team Sports (football, baseball, basketball, etc.)				
24. Camping				
25. Traveling				
26. Gardening				
27. Peace and Quiet				
28. Other items that give you pleasure:				
_____				
_____				

Week 1: Self-monitoring. In order to start changing poor eating habits, first you must identify your current eating habits. In your small notebook, make charts like the illustration on page 23. Make entries exact. Time and feelings: 5:17 P.M., bored, angry, etc. Place and with whom you ate: kitchen, alone or Joe's Cafe, Dad. Amount: 1 oz., 1 cup, etc. Type of food and how prepared: chicken breast—fried in oil.

Include everything you put in your mouth except water, and that means the margarine on your bread, the cream in your coffee and the dressing on your salad. Fill in the chart either right before or immediately after eating. Be accurate—even when you overeat. Keeping this kind of chart works best when you turn it in regularly to a physician, psychologist or dietitian.

FOOD RECORD*

Name__Mary Jones_____

Meal Plan___The Take-It-Off Plan_____Date___June 5____

2	Dairy Delights_____
2+	Ad Lib Veggies_____
1	Limited Veggies_____
3	Nature's Treats_____
4	Complex Carbs_____
5	Protein Providers____
3	Palate Pleasers_____
2	Flexi-Foods_____
2	Soup Group_____

Write ONE food on each line.

Time/ Feelings	Place/ Who With	Amount	Food—How Prepared	Food Group
7:30 A.M./	Kitchen/	1	Poached egg	Protein Providers—1
Neutral	John	1 slice	Whole wheat toast, dry	Complex Carbs—1
		1 small	Orange	Nature's Treats—1

*Adapted from form developed by the Diet Modification Clinic, Baylor College of Medicine and The Methodist Hospital.

If it seems tedious or boring at first, take heart. It's easier after the first month, and many patients later say that keeping a chart was the single most beneficial component of the "behavior mod" program. In addition to giving you an awareness of how much you eat and an idea of your dietary life-style, the simple act of writing in itself has a positive effect on your diet plan.

The second thing to keep track of is your body weight. Buy graph paper and hang it in a prominent, visible place, preferably near the scales. Weigh yourself every day at the same time, and mark it on a graph that lists pounds (in one-pound increments) down the left side, and days of the month (1 through 31) along the bottom (see illustration, page 25). Don't be concerned with daily fluctuations of a pound or two. This is normal.

You should have one graph for every month. This process is useful because it keeps you aware of your weight at all times during the program. Many obese people avoid the scales when they suspect they're gaining weight, so the graph serves as an objective reminder should you start to slip.

Week 2: Control Your Eating Environment. First, choose one place to eat when you're at home (the dining room, the kitchen, etc.), and eat every meal there. The only exception is when you're drinking coffee, plain tea, water or other calorie-free beverage. Second, don't do anything else while eating. No TV, letters, newspapers or phone calls. Concentrate fully on eating. Third, join the "dirty-plate club." Leave at least one bite of food on your plate at the end of each meal. If it's hard to remember, make a little sign saying "leave a bite."

Week 3: Control and Change of Food Consumption. Learn to eat slowly and enjoy your food. If you eat hot soup before a meal, you tend to eat more slowly. When you come to the main course, chew and savor each bite. Lay down your utensils between bites and only pick them up when you have completely chewed and swallowed the previous one.

Stop and take a break when you are one-third to one-half the way through your meal. The rationale behind all these suggestions is simple. It takes 20 minutes for the body to feel satisfied once you start eating. The longer you take to eat, the less food it will take to make you feel full.[4]

Try to do without seconds. The best way to achieve this is to serve yourself and your family in the kitchen, rather than putting a full, tempting bowl of fragrant food on the table right in front of you.

THE SOUP DIET DAILY WEIGHT GRAPH*

Name __Mary Jones__   Month __June__

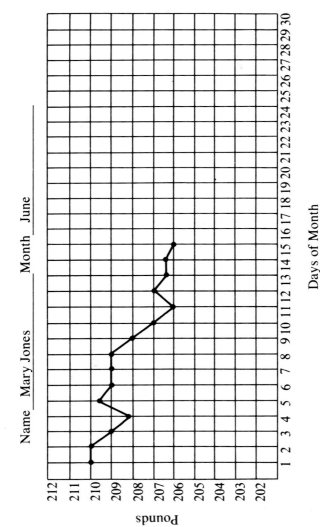

Days of Month

*Adapted from form developed by the Diet Modification Clinic, Baylor College of Medicine and
The Methodist Hospital.

Finally, use a slightly smaller plate and spread the food out over it. This makes your single serving appear larger.

Week 4: Control of Eating Cues. First, store all food out of sight to cut down on snacking. Second, foods in the refrigerator should be kept in opaque containers instead of clear glass bottles that reveal all the tempting food inside. You may even want to turn out the bulb in the fridge! Third, don't nibble while you cook. You can help yourself in this by chewing gum, wearing a surgical mask or brushing your teeth before food preparation. It's also a good idea to prepare foods when you're not hungry. For example, pack lunches after dinner rather than before breakfast. Finally, if possible, have someone else scrape the dishes and put away the leftovers. If you live alone, put extra food away before you sit down to eat the meal and afterwards, scrape your plate directly into the garbage. Remember: no snacking!

Week 5: Control of Obtaining Food. Don't overload your digestive system by eating the whole day's calorie allowance at one meal. Eat three meals a day. Also, go shopping only once a week, using a prepared menu plan. Shop after a meal when you're not hungry, never before one. And put the grocery bags in the trunk or on the back seat to avoid the temptation to snack.

Week 6: Control of Indiscriminate Eating. Make a list of activities you enjoy—hobbies, reading, music, sports or movies. You can even make another list of things you must do: pay bills, do chores, clean a closet, do laundry. Keep these lists in plain view, and when you feel you want to go on a food binge, consciously choose an alternative activity instead. If you must eat, binge on lettuce, celery or cucumbers. It helps to avoid keeping "junk" food or high-calorie snack foods around. If you want to binge because you're feeling tired, take a nap. If you want to overeat because you are angry, bored, depressed or under a lot of stress, try this relaxation technique. You can easily teach yourself the technique within three weeks if you do it twice a day, 15 minutes a session.

RELAXATION TECHNIQUE

Find a quiet place away from the telephone and family. Sit in a comfortable chair and loosen tight clothing. Turn down the lights and close your eyes, letting the cares of the day disappear for a few minutes.

With your eyes closed, imagine yourself on a bridge looking down on a black stream of water that's slowly flowing away from you. Now, imagine a bright, clear, white light on top of this water. As it moves downstream, it gets smaller and smaller. As it diminishes in size, it seems to get brighter, and as it brightens it starts to spin. As it becomes smaller and brighter and harder to look at, you find yourself relaxing. Your arms and your eyelids grow very heavy. Begin counting to ten very slowly. One, you are very calm. Two, you're starting to go into a dreamlike state. Three, you're very peaceful. Four, you're beginning to drift. Five, you're slowly drifting. Six, you're drifting, feeling relaxed. Seven, eight, drifting. Nine, ten, relax.

You are now in a state of complete relaxation. You are feeling very calm and secure. It is peaceful here. Stay in this state about five minutes. Don't worry if thoughts start to intrude. When you notice distractions, just calmly turn your attention to the movement of breath at your nostrils.

After five minutes, begin counting backward from three to one. When you reach one, you will feel relaxed, but not at all tired. Open your eyes, and move your arms and legs. You're feeling very refreshed.

Week 7: Contingency Contracting. Make a contract that will be signed by you and a friend or relative (see example, page 29). Write today's date, and indicate that the life of the contract is for one month from today.

Now, give the other signee a predetermined amount of money. Then, write that for each pound of weight you lose, you will be paid back ''x'' amount. The idea is to try to lose one to two pounds a week. At the end of the month, all remaining money will be sent by your friend to an organization you dislike. If all the money has been returned to you, you are allowed to spend the money on a present—a new hat, or a record, or whatever. Figure out all the details and write them in the contract before you begin.

The Soup Diet Conditional Contract

A formal contract will provide additional motivation to help you carry out those good intentions of losing weight. Here's how it is done:

1. Choose an organization that you strongly dislike. It might be a political party or candidate, the booster club of a rival high school or college or a political movement you oppose. This organization will benefit if you fail to lose weight.

2. Then complete *The Soup Diet Take-It-Off Contract* on the next page. Write in today's date and your name as "party of the first part" on the first two lines. Write in the name of your spouse, other family member or close friend who has agreed to help you in your weight program as "party of the second part." In the space preceded by the dollar sign write in the total sum you wish to pledge. Under item 1 write in the date four weeks from today. After the words "shall be paid to" in item 2, write in the name of the organization you chose as the one you dislike.

3. Under item 3, write in a reward for meeting your goal. This might be a new dress, a record, a concert, a weekend trip, etc. The Soup Diet Pleasure Chart might help give you ideas for your "reward." Although your reward doesn't have to cost a lot of money, it should be something "extra-special." After all, a month's weight loss takes a lot of work. Give it some thought, talk with your "party of the second part," and try to come up with something that will really be rewarding to you.

4. At the bottom of the contract the "party of the second part," two family members or friends ("witnesses") and yourself should sign.

5. Now work towards losing the weight. After the expiration date, you may then wish to renegotiate a new contract for more pounds. Never negotiate a contract for more than ten pounds at any one time; chances are, it won't work. To work effectively, a contract should also cover only a fairly short time period, such as four to five weeks.

It has been our experience that contracts work very well for some people. If you truly want to lose weight, the contract will serve as an additional motivator while you are working on the behavioral techniques discussed in this book.

THE SOUP DIET
TAKE-IT-OFF CONTRACT*

KNOW ALL INDIVIDUALS BY THESE PRESENTS:

This contract made and entered into this _____ day of _____, 19 ___, by and between _____ hereinafter called party of the first part and _____ hereinafter called party of the second part, witnesseth:

For and in consideration of the mutual promises contained, said parties agree as follows:

I, the party of the first part, agree to deposit the total sum of $_____ in cash, with the party of the second part. This sum represents a commitment of $_____ per pound which shall be held by the party of the second part until disbursed according to the following conditions:

1. I, party of the first part, agree to work hard to lose weight by faithfully following the principles of the Soup Diet Take-It-Off Plan and will try to lose one to two pounds per week. For each pound of body weight that I have lost from the date of this agreement until the _____ day of _____, 19 ___, I will be paid back $_____ per pound of my deposit. The total amount so returned will not exceed the total amount I have paid to the party of the second part.

2. All money remaining on deposit with the party of the second part shall be paid to _____.

3. If the full sum of money is returned to the party of the first part, the party of the second part agrees to:
   a. Praise lavishly the party of the first part for achieving the weight loss.
   b. Reward the party of the first part by _____ _____.

We have both read the terms and conditions of the above contract and agree to them as written.

_____   _____
Party of the first part   Party of the second part

_____   _____
Witness   Witness

Weight on date contract made _____

Weight on date contract ends _____

*Adapted from form developed by the Diet Modification Clinic, Baylor College of Medicine and The Methodist Hospital.

Week 8: Control When Eating Away From Home. If you eat out often, try to frequent the same restaurant where you are a regular customer and where they will know your portion needs. Keep your eating plan in mind when you order:

—*meats* should be trimmed of all fat, and broiled without fat. The best choices are chops, steak, chicken or fish.
—*vegetables* that are buttered, creamed or prepared in cheese sauces should be avoided.
—*salads* should not be ordered with cheese or cream-style dressings.
—*fats* should be limited according to your eating plan.
—*breads* should not be used to fill up while waiting for the main course. Nibble on raw vegetables instead.
—*beverages* such as skim milk, vegetable or fruit juices, coffee or tea are the best.
—*desserts* include fresh or unsweetened fruit or try a cup of hot coffee or tea instead.

If you're in a restaurant and served a food not on your eating plan, douse it with pepper to avoid eating it, or ask that it be removed from the table. If you're going to a party, eat before going. Once there, fill up on vegetables and salad. If there's a buffet, avoid conversation areas near the table. Carry your plate to the opposite side of the room. Instead of having too many drinks, sip slowly on club soda or mineral water with a lemon wedge. Talk more, eat less.

Week 9: Maintaining Ideal Weight. Continue keeping your food record for one month after reaching your goal weight. Always weigh yourself daily and enter the number on the graph. If you creep up five pounds, review the weekly lessons and start again. If you know you're going on vacation or a major holiday is approaching, lose weight beforehand in anticipation. If you come into a period of stress in your life, don't add to your problems by trying to lose more weight. During times of difficulty, just "aim to maintain."

Give away or tailor the clothes that are too large. Don't keep them around as a temptation to return to your old size. Purchase some new, attractive clothes that fit well.

Allow yourself to be vain. Now that you're at your ideal weight, glory in it. Dress up every chance you get. Notice how people are reacting differently to you. Remind yourself of all the work it took to reach your ideal weight and don't let that effort be wasted. Care about yourself.

Congratulations! You've carried through a nine-week behavior modification plan on your own. You may have had a friend or therapist offer assistance—but you have succeeded on your own!

III

The Diet/Exercise Connection

by KIM STAMBAUGH

"If exercise could be packed into a pill, it would be the single most widely prescribed, and beneficial, medicine in the Nation."

—Robert N. Butler, M.D.
Director
National Institute on Aging

Conventional wisdom says inside every fat person is a thin person clamoring to get out. What it fails to mention is that the new, thinner you will be saggy and flabby if you don't exercise while you diet. Like an oversized coat, your "skin" will be the wrong size.

A thin person—flabby? Listen to what happened to one of my students who went from 175 to 130 pounds in five months. Jenni faithfully exercised as she dropped the first 35 pounds, and looked better week by week. Then an illness restricted further activity, and she lost the final 10 pounds without exercise.

"I was the thinnest I had ever been," she said. "Yet my skin was literally hanging on my body. It was worse than being overweight because it looked so unsightly!"

Besides refitting your skin to the thinner you, exercise also helps you lose weight. In order to lose one pound you have to burn off 3500 calories more than you take in. This is true whether you're munching carrot sticks or simply cutting back on desserts: your daily energy output (exercise and activity) must exceed your daily calorie intake (eating and drinking). Daily physical exercise can increase your energy output and help you lose weight without restricting calories severely.

What follows is a chart illustrating the energy expenditure

ENERGY EXPENDITURE CHART

The following chart shows you how many calories you may expend engaging in one or more of these physical activities. The chart also shows how easily you can replace those calories. Both exercise *and* diet are important for weight control.

ACTIVITY	APPROXIMATE NUMBER OF CALORIES USED PER HOUR	APPROXIMATE AMOUNT OF FOOD
Lying down or sleeping	80	1 peach half in heavy syrup
Sitting	100	8 oz. cola drink
Driving an automobile	120	12 jellybeans
Standing	140	15 potato chips
Domestic work	180	4 vanilla sandwich cookies
Walking, 2½ mph	210	1 frozen waffle and 2 tablespoons maple syrup
Bicycling, 5½ mph	210	2 tablespoons mayonnaise
Gardening	220	1 cup hot chocolate
Golf, lawn mowing, power mower	250	2 fried chicken thighs
Bowling	270	1 hot dog
Walking, 3¾ mph	300	¾ cup hash browns
Swimming, ½ mph	300	1 cup soft ice cream
Square dancing, volleyball; roller skating	350	1 slice layer cake
Wood chopping or sawing	400	4 oz. corned beef
Tennis	420	1 cup French fries
Skiing, 10 mph	600	1 double-decker hamburger
Squash and handball	600	1 fried fish sandwich with tartar sauce
Bicycling, 13 mph	660	1 slice apple pie topped with 2 scoops vanilla ice cream
Running, 10 mph	900	1 large chocolate malt

Figures are for a 150-pound person. Activity energy figures based on material prepared by Robert E. Johnson, M.D., Ph.D., and colleagues, University of Illinois. Amounts of foods based on figures obtained from USDA Handbook No. 456 and analyses from various fast-food restaurants.

required to *stay even with* the calories of selected foods. Remember that the figures are approximations. Heavier people burn more calories than lighter people doing the same exercise.

One of the most important reasons to exercise while dieting is to reshape and tone the muscles. The upper body is the first area to lose weight: the cheeks hollow, then the neck and chin become loose, the skin under the arms becomes fleshy and finally the waist becomes soft. If you exercise as these areas readjust to your new weight, they will become firm instead of flabby.

It is a myth that while dieting you will be too weak to engage in strenuous activities. In fact, exercise is an energizer. It can keep your body strong and flexible as your weight redistributes itself and can increase your resistance to fatigue.

It's also a misconception that when you are physically active you are hungrier. Though some people feel hungrier at the start of an exercise program, scientists blame this on expectation more than anything else. Many people actually eat less once they become physically fit.

There are psychological benefits to exercising, too. Some people become anxious or depressed during months of dieting and what seems to be unending privation. Exercising lifts your spirits, gives you something positive to focus on. Exercise also boosts your self-image. It's a signal that you're back in control and actively doing something about your weight.

I believe that exercise also increases your awareness about your body, so that as time goes on you notice slight changes better than you did before. If you slip on your diet and gain a pound or two, your newly sensitized body lets you know immediately.

In order to get the most from exercise, you have to make a firm commitment to it and not stop once your diet ends. Exercise must become a regular part of your life, like brushing your teeth.

Hour-long classes at least twice a week are the absolute minimum if you are to gain any benefits; four one-hour sessions a week are preferable if you really want to drop that body fat. If regular classes don't conform to your schedule, even a 15- to 20-minute workout at home every day can bring benefits. Remember, if burning calories is your goal, frequent exercise at a moderate pace for extended sessions is more effective than occasional, short workouts at a hard-driving pace.

Enjoying the form of exercise you choose is as important as doing it. If exercise is pure torture, you'll lose interest. But if exercising is a joy, you'll try harder, won't give up easily and will look forward to the good feeling you know it brings.

In deciding on a form of exercise, ask yourself what you're trying to accomplish. In other words, what are your needs? If you're already in fairly good shape and only have a pound or two to lose, you may want a maintenance form of exercise, such as golf, tennis, softball or some other sport.

If you want to strengthen your cardiovascular system and burn calories to lose weight, think in terms of aerobic dancing, jazz classes, vigorous walking, running, swimming, bicycling, jumping rope, cross-country skiing or using a mini-trampoline. Calisthenics can be included on this list as long as you don't stop to rest between exercises. The key to "fat burning" activity is to choose an exercise that is repetitive, rhythmic and can be done continuously for at least 30 minutes to an hour. These are called "aerobic" exercises because they require you to breathe in more oxygen as your muscles work harder, your heart beats faster and your breathing becomes deeper.

If your goal is to reshape specific body parts and lose inches in certain strategic areas, an exercise class that emphasizes stretching would be ideal. Weight lifting is good spot exercise for arms and leg muscles.

If meeting people and socializing are high priorities, then classes at the Y or a local community center seem a good choice. Hate smelly gyms and like being outdoors and running in the woods? Prefer to work out indoors where the vagaries of weather won't interfere with your schedule? These seemingly obvious questions should be answered before you settle on the proper exercise program so that once you've started, you'll be less tempted to quit.

An ideal regimen for someone trying to lose weight is the combination of an active, aerobic sport with a regular class that focuses on stretching, spot exercises and flexibility.

Before beginning any exercise program, you should seek medical approval, particularly if you are elderly or have a chronic disease or long-standing injury. People with injuries—bad backs, weak knees, shin splints or arthritic hips—should stay away from jogging or running and seek out gentler body shapers, such as swimming or using the mini-trampoline.

When beginning an exercise program, work out at a slower pace at first and know your limitations. If you are in a class, don't compete with your classmates.

Whatever form of exercise you choose, you'll want some

way to measure whether you're exercising hard enough, and whether you're improving over time.

To determine if you're benefiting from aerobic exercises, first calculate your maximum heart rate, which is the number of beats your heart makes per minute when it is working at its fullest capacity. Although it varies depending on age, sex and fitness level, your maximum heart rate is roughly 220 minus your age. For example, if you're 30, it's about 190. (For a more precise measurement, take a treadmill test at your doctor's office.)

It would be dangerous for most people to exercise at their maximum heart rate. The most efficient level for exercise is called the "target heart rate range." You can calculate the lower end of this range by multiplying your maximum heart rate by 70 percent. The higher end is figured by multiplying your maximum heart rate by 85 percent. For example, the 30-year-old with a maximum heart rate of 190 would have a target heart rate range of 133 to 162.

Once you have determined your target heart rate range, you will want to measure your actual heartbeats while exercising. After about 15 minutes of working out, take your pulse for a count of six seconds (take your pulse either at your wrist or gently at your neck) and multiply that number of beats by ten. If your heart is beating within your target range, you are exercising efficiently and burning anywhere from 8 to 12 calories per minute, depending on your body size. If you are below or above your target range, adjust your exercise pace as necessary.

Stretching and strengthening exercises need different benchmarks from aerobic exercises. You'll need to measure effectiveness and progress through flexibility, endurance and efficiency.

Flexibility is the ease with which muscle groups lengthen and contract, which in turn determines range of movement. You can measure your flexibility before and after a specific exercise session, or periodically to see how you progress over a course of time. To measure back and hamstring flexibility, see how far you can bend over to touch your toes, without forcing the stretch. Waist flexibility can be determined by doing side bends from a standing position, without bouncing. Hip flexion is measured by trying to bring your knee to your chest from a standing position, keeping your back straight and balancing with your other hand on a counter top.

Endurance is the ability to sustain movement for a given length of time without tiring or changing pace. You can improve your endurance level over time by increasing the number of repetitions for each exercise you perform. For example, you may start with 8 side bends, and increase to 16 the following week.

Efficiency is the ability to expend the proper amount of energy—not too much or too little—for a given movement. Beginners often put too much effort into exercises, thereby wasting energy and causing strain and injury. You don't lose more calories by pushing too hard. You are efficient when you feel energized, not depleted, after exercising.

For those of us who are rushed and can't find as much time to exercise as we would like, mini-exercises can be integrated into daily life that are excellent spot shapers. Though they shouldn't replace regular, vigorous exercise, they're a good use of idle moments:

—for thighs: While waiting for a bus or in line at the grocery store, tighten buttocks, press thighs together, hold for a few seconds and release. For subtlety's sake, not recommended in tight jeans!

—for calves: While waiting, simply raise your heels in the air and come up on your toes. Lower your heels back down and repeat several times—first with both feet together, then alternating feet.

—for legs/stomach: In a high, straight back chair at work (not a secretarial office chair), slide your rear all the way in, so you're against the back of the chair. Place hands on arms of chair, and keeping back straight and abdomen in, lift one leg, slightly-bent, off chair. Hold, release and alternate to other leg. Repeat several times. The secret of this exercise—which my 92-year-old grandfather swears by—is keeping the base of your spine and lower back up against the back of the chair. If you slide forward, it's too easy.

—for legs/stomach: Waiting at the kitchen counter for the coffee to perk, do leg swings back and forth, keeping your back straight as you swing. First swing one leg about five times, then the other. Beginners and people with back problems should swing the leg bent; advanced exercisers can keep the leg straight.

EXERCISES

As fun as these "quickie" exercises can be, to truly reshape your body during weight loss you'll need to put out sweat and effort. The following exercises concentrate on the most common trouble spots for dieters. For each problem area we offer an exercise for beginners and one for more advanced exercisers:

1. **Face/Neck**
    A. BEGINNERS
       Tilt head back, bringing chin forward. Make exaggerated chewing movements with mouth.

    B. ADVANCED
       Tilt head back, open eyes and mouth wide. Now scrunch eyes closed while wrapping lips around teeth. Alternate.

2. **Arms/Upper Back/Bust**

A. BEGINNERS

Stand with feet spread a bit wider than hips' width, toes pointed forward. Lift arms straight out from shoulders. Flex hands upward as much as possible and pull in stomach. Twist at the waist from right to left over and over. Allow head to twist from side to side as you move.

B. ADVANCED

Stand with feet spread wider than hips' width, toes pointed forward and arms straight out from shoulders as in A. Lean over from hips, keeping back as straight as possible. Make fists. Lower arms down towards floor so thumbs almost touch one another. Now, open arms out to side again in flapping motion, as if you were flying. Remaining bent over, continue lowering and lifting arms with strong, swinging movements for a total of 15 counts. Return to standing position, rest and repeat series.

3. **Waist**

A. BEGINNERS

Stand with feet shoulder-width apart, toes pointed forward, knees slightly bent. Tuck pelvis under and pull stomach in. Extend left arm over head by ear, and put right hand on hip. Bend right as far as feels comfortable and bounce gently eight times, feeling the stretch in the left side. Arm should remain straight over head. Repeat same movement eight times to left. Repeat both sides several times.

B. ADVANCED

Assume same starting position as above. However, interlace fingers, turn palms upward and extend both arms straight up over head. Keeping pelvis tucked under, bend slowly to right as far as you can, then return to upright position. Repeat to left, keeping stomach pulled in and knees bent. Repeat series four times.

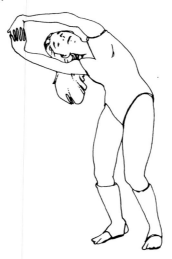

4. **Hips/Thighs**

A. BEGINNERS

Lie on right side, extend legs and support head by hand and elbow. Raise left leg to 45-degree angle, flexing foot at ankle and keeping toes and knee facing forward. Keeping left knee straight and buttocks tight, lower left leg to meet right leg, then return left leg to 45-degree angle. Repeat sequence at a snappy pace for 24 counts. Repeat sequence on left side, using right leg.

B. ADVANCED

Stand with legs together, toes pointed forward, with hand on a bar, kitchen counter or top of a chair. Back should be straight and abdomen pulled in. Beginning with outside leg, lift knee upward to hip level, toe pointed downward. Return leg to starting position. Extend same leg directly out to side with foot flexed at ankle. Keeping knee straight and buttocks tight, return leg to standing position. Repeat sequence ten times for each leg.

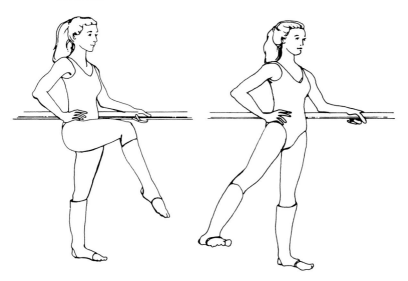

5. **Abdomen**

A. BEGINNERS

Lie on back with knees bent into chest. Put hands under buttocks, palms facing down, to support lower back. Keeping small of back on floor at all times and stomach pulled in, make a bicycling action with the legs. Keep feet as close to the floor as possible. Bicycle for ten counts. Rest and repeat for at least two more sets.

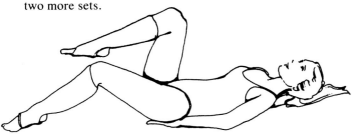

B. ADVANCED

Same exercise as above, except instead of putting hands under buttocks, interlace fingers behind head. Lift head and shoulders from the floor, hugging elbows to ears. Keeping lower back on floor and stomach pulled in, make bicycle legs for a count of 20. Rest and repeat.

6. **Buttocks**

A. BEGINNERS

Lie with back on floor, knees bent and feet about as wide apart as hips. Toes should be slightly turned out. Raise hips several inches from floor, taking care not to arch back. Squeeze buttocks muscles together tightly and gently bounce hips up and down for 10 counts. Lower hips and return to floor, rolling spine down slowly, vertebra by vertebra. Repeat for at least two more sets.

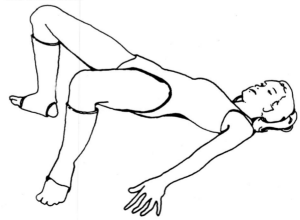

B. ADVANCED

Kneel on all fours with arms directly under shoulders. Keeping back straight, extend right leg straight back. Touch the floor with the side of the right big toe. Lift this leg upward until buttocks tighten, taking care to keep knee straight. Now lower leg to floor and repeat this lift/lower pattern for 24 counts. Maintain a quick, steady pace. Rest and repeat with same leg for 24 counts, then switch to other leg.

IV

Designing
Your Own Diet

Now that you know the benefits of regular exercise and have decided you are ready to start your diet, it's time to learn about the Soup Diet.

The Soup Diet provides three plans: the Kick-Off Diet, the Take-It-Off Plan and the Keep-It-Off-Forever Plan. You do not count calories in any of the plans. The Kick-Off Diet provides you with ten days of menus that you should follow exactly. Featuring separate calorie levels for both men and women, the Take-It-Off and Keep-It-Off-Forever Plans use groups of foods from which you choose a specified number of servings daily.

Designed to help you lose weight quickly, the Kick-Off Diet gives you the incentive you need to go on to the Take-It-Off and Keep-It-Off-Forever Plans. As Dr. Foreyt has shown, rewards in dieting are extremely important, and what could be more rewarding than losing weight? To give you best results, the Kick-Off Diet cuts calories to a minimum while still giving you nutritionally valuable meals. However, sensitive to the hunger pangs you may experience on such a low-calorie intake and knowing from studies that soup can help slow your eating pace (which helps you to eat fewer calories yet still gain the satisfying feeling of having eaten enough), the Kick-Off Diet specifies three servings of soup per day. Many soups are also "nutritionally dense" foods, meaning they provide a high level of nutrients compared to the calories they contain, making those soups a wise choice for any dieter. On the Take-It-Off Plan, soup appears twice daily to help ease the pain of dieting and to make a significant contribution to your nutrient intake.

The Keep-It-Off-Forever Plan features soup once a day as a way to keep your calorie intake under control when you're not dieting.

Besides helping you to lose or maintain your weight, the Soup Diet plans also help control nutrients that medical researchers now counsel us to reduce in our diets. Since fat is high in calories (9 calories per gram compared to 4 calories per gram of protein or carbohydrate), it must be limited in any weight-control program. But also because of its possible role in the development of heart disease and cancer, researchers recommend we reduce our fat consumption from the typical American intake of about 40 percent of total calories to about 30 percent or one-third of your total calories.[8] The Soup Diet plans stay within that level. Saturated fat and cholesterol intake is also controlled within advised levels.

Although recommendations state we should increase the amount of carbohydrate in our diet, the amount of the carbohydrate sugar should be limited. Americans now consume an average of one-quarter of their total calories from sugar daily.[8] The Soup Diet allows sugar on both the Take-It-Off and Keep-It-Off-Forever Plans but limits its use well within the current recommendation of 15 percent of total caloric intake (about one-sixth of total calories). The remainder of our carbohydrate intake should come from fruits and vegetables and grain products.[8] The Soup Diet provides plenty of these foods that help keep you from being hungry and go far towards meeting your vitamin and mineral needs.

Americans are estimated to consume between four and ten grams of sodium per day. In 1980 the Department of Health and Human Services set as a goal for most adults no more than three to six grams of sodium per day.[9] The Soup Diet Take-It-Off and Keep-It-Off-Forever Plans limit sodium to about three grams. The Kick-Off Diet menus total about four grams per day.

The Soup Diet eating plans were designed by registered dietitians to provide levels of nutrients as specified by the U.S. Recommended Daily Allowances (U.S. RDA). All menus and recipes were checked for nutritional adequacy and calorie counts by computer analysis. However, since diets below 1800 calories may be low in vitamins and minerals, a daily vitamin and mineral supplement (with iron for women) providing 100 percent of the U.S. RDA is advised when following the Kick-Off Diet and the Take-It-Off Plan.[10]

You should begin the Soup Diet with the Kick-Off Diet on page 54. After ten days, go on to the Take-It-Off Plan, following it until you and your doctor decide you have reached your ideal weight. Be sure to read the Introduction to the Soup Diet Food Groups, which begins on page 78 before starting the Take-It-Off Plan. If you reach your ideal weight after following the Kick-Off Diet for ten days, follow the Take-It-Off Plan for at least two weeks to stabilize your weight.

To help you maintain your weight loss, progress to the Keep-It-Off-Forever Plan. The Keep-It-Off-Forever Plan gives you a guide for nutritious eating you can follow for the rest of your life.

IT'S TIME TO GET STARTED!

Now that you understand the Soup Diet, it's time to get started. Just follow these eight easy steps:

1. Check with your doctor to be sure it is safe for you to begin the diet.
2. Follow the Kick-Off Diet for ten days. Keep daily food records to get used to them and become aware of your eating habits.
3. Meanwhile, study the Soup Diet Food Groups to familiarize yourself with allowed foods and portion sizes.
4. After ten days of the Kick-Off Diet, move on to the Take-It-Off Plan.
5. Learn the total servings your plan requires from each Soup Diet Food Group.
6. Study the sample menus for your plan and design your own menus.
7. Continue to work with food records to closely monitor your intake and eating habits.
8. Begin the Soup Diet with your next meal.
HAPPY EATING!

THE KICK-OFF DIET

The Soup Diet Kick-Off Diet is designed to be a ten-day program. Menus provide about 1000 calories per day. There is no need for you to count calories, but you should follow the menus exactly as shown. You may change the order of days if you'd like, but it is important you do not eat from the same menu every day. As with any diet, you should not attempt to follow the Kick-Off Diet without first consulting your physician.

Fill out a food record daily as Dr. Foreyt described in Chapter II to become familiar with using the form and become aware of your eating habits. Be sure to fill it out exactly even when your menu differs from the Kick-Off Diet menu.

Day 6 and Day 7 menus are designed so you can stay on your diet easily through the weekend. Recipes for items starred in the menus are found at the end of the menu section.

Tips to help you easily follow and obtain the most benefit from the Kick-Off Diet include:

- Trim all meats of visible fat and remove skin from poultry.
- Quantities for meats, fish or poultry indicate weight after cooking.
- All vegetables are "free," unless an amount is specified.
- Use fresh or frozen vegetables.
- Use fresh, canned or dried fruits or fruit juices, prepared without sugar.
- Cook foods without added fat unless indicated. Use nonstick cookware or nonstick cooking sprays.
- It is not necessary to weigh or measure foods if you can accurately estimate amounts. If you can't judge accurately, try weighing and measuring for the first few days until you learn correct portion sizes.
- Mark your favorite glass with pieces of tape to show the levels of common amounts of liquid (*i.e.*, ⅓ cup, ½ cup or 4 ounces, ¾ cup or 6 ounces).
- Soups should be reconstituted only with water unless otherwise specified.
- Black coffee and teas and calorie-free beverages can be used freely.

- Use only skim milk that has been fortified with vitamins A and D.
- If you're dieting solo, you will have leftovers when you use the recipes. Divide the leftovers into individual servings and freeze each separately for later use in the Take-It-Off Plan. You'll find the Food Group Equivalents on page 175 will help you plan your daily menus.

KICK-OFF DIET MENUS

Day 1

BREAKFAST OR MIDMORNING SNACK
½ small banana sliced over ⅓ cup bran buds covered with
½ cup frosty cold skim milk
Steaming hot coffee or tea

LUNCH
1 cup prepared Campbell's Won Ton Soup garnished with
   radish slices and chopped parsley
2 ounces chilled white-meat tuna (water-pack) on bed of crisp
   lettuce garnished with onion brushes, tomato wedges and
   lemon slice
4 slices crisp thin flatbread wafers
Bubbly mineral water over ice with slice of fresh lime

SNACK
1 serving Fruit Creme*

DINNER
1 cup prepared Campbell's Chicken with Rice Soup
2 ounces fresh, roasted chicken without skin, cooked with
   thyme
Lightly steamed broccoli spears
1 small warmed dinner roll
¾ cup chilled unsweetened fresh or frozen strawberries covered with
¼ cup frosty cold evaporated skim milk
Steaming hot coffee or tea

SNACK
1 cup prepared Campbell's Consommé (Beef) Soup
Crunchy raw vegetable platter of carrot sticks, cucumber slices
   and green pepper rings

Lunch: Won Ton Soup, Tuna Salad with Flatbread & Mineral Water

Day 2

BREAKFAST OR MIDMORNING SNACK

⅓ cup chilled ''V-8'' Cocktail Vegetable Juice over ice with slice of fresh lemon

1 slice crisp whole wheat toast spread with ¼ cup part-skim ricotta cheese flavored with ¼ teaspoon vanilla extract

Steaming hot coffee or tea

LUNCH

1 cup prepared Campbell's Chicken with Rice Soup

Cottage Cheese and Fresh Fruit Parfait (½ cup lowfat cottage cheese layered with ½ cup unsweetened mixed fruit, such as apples, peaches, plums, pineapple or citrus, etc.)

2 slices crunchy melba toast

Bubbly mineral water with slice of fresh lime

SNACK

½ cup plain lowfat yogurt flavored with ¼ teaspoon orange extract and a pinch of ground nutmeg

DINNER

1 cup prepared Campbell's Oyster Stew Soup, made with ½ cup skim milk

1 serving Vegetable Scramble*

1 small sliced potato sautéed with 1 small minced garlic clove in nonstick skillet

½ cup crisp shredded carrots mixed with ¼ cup juicy cold unsweetened crushed pineapple and 1 tablespoon chewy raisins

½ cup frosty cold skim milk

Steaming hot coffee or tea

SNACK

1 cup prepared Campbell's Crispy Spanish Style Vegetable Soup

1 serving Herbed Croutons*

Day 3

BREAKFAST OR MIDMORNING SNACK
1/2 cup chilled juicy unsweetened orange sections mixed with
1/4 cup lowfat cottage cheese
1 slice crisp whole wheat toast
Steaming hot coffee or tea

LUNCH
Open-faced Tuna and Tomato Sandwich (1 slice fresh whole
    wheat bread spread with tuna salad made with 1 1/2 ounces
    tuna mixed with 1 teaspoon mayonnaise, 1 teaspoon
    chopped celery and 1 teaspoon chopped green pepper and
    topped with 1 thin slice tomato)
1 cup frosty cold skim milk

SNACK
1 cup prepared Campbell's Won Ton Soup
3/4 cup Polar Berries (unsweetened frozen strawberries)

DINNER
1 cup prepared Campbell's Consommé (Beef) Soup
1 serving Marvelous Manicotti*
Steamed fresh or frozen asparagus spears with sliced fresh
    mushrooms
Crisp tossed salad with lettuce, carrots, cucumbers and lemon
    wedge
Butter Rum Froth (1 cup frosty cold skim milk blended with 1/2
    teaspoon rum extract and 1/2 teaspoon butter extract)
Steaming hot coffee or tea

SNACK
1 cup prepared Campbell's Crispy Spanish Style Soup
Crisp chilled cucumber rounds

Day 4

BREAKFAST OR MIDMORNING SNACK

⅓ cup bran buds topped with 3 chopped dried unsweetened
apricot halves and covered with ½ cup frosty cold skim milk
Steaming hot coffee or tea

LUNCH

1 cup prepared Campbell's Old Fashioned Vegetable Soup
1 Individual Pita Pizza*
Crispy fresh bean sprouts marinated in red wine vinegar with a
pinch of basil
½ cup juicy unsweetened pineapple chunks garnished with
fresh mint sprigs
Lemony iced tea

SNACK

Chilled crunchy cauliflowerets with 1 serving Cucumber
Yogurt Dip*

DINNER

1 cup prepared Campbell's Oyster Stew Soup, made with ½
cup skim milk
1 serving Hawaiian Chicken Kabobs*
½ cup hot and fluffy brown rice cooked with basil
Mixed crispy lettuce and spinach leaves with lemon wedge
Steaming hot coffee or tea

SNACK

1 cup prepared Campbell's Chicken & Stars Soup
Crunchy celery sticks

Dinner: Broiled Lamb Chops, Stuffed Tomatoes, Old Fashioned
Vegetable Soup & Coffee

Day 5

BREAKFAST OR MIDMORNING SNACK

¾ cup crunchy whole-grain flake cereal with 2 tablespoons
   chewy raisins covered with 1 cup frosty cold skim milk
Steaming hot coffee or tea

LUNCH

1 cup prepared Campbell's Beef Broth Soup
1 serving Curried Cauliflower Polonaise*
½ cup chilled unsweetened fruit cup (mix peaches, pears,
   plums, citrus, etc.)
Bubbly cold mineral water with slice of fresh lime

SNACK

Cappuccino Cooler (1 cup frosty cold skim milk with 1 teaspoon instant coffee)

DINNER

1 cup prepared Campbell's Old Fashioned Vegetable Soup
2 tender broiled lamb chops (2¾″ × 2″ × 1¼″ each)
1 serving Rice Stuffed Tomatoes*
Steaming hot coffee or tea

SNACK

1 cup prepared Campbell's Chicken Gumbo Soup
2 slices crunchy melba toast

Day 6

BREAKFAST OR MIDMORNING SNACK
1 fresh grapefruit half
2 Spiced Whole Wheat Pancakes* covered with Almond
  Yogurt Topping (6 tablespoons lowfat yogurt with ½ teaspoon almond extract)
Steaming hot coffee or tea

LUNCH
1 cup prepared Campbell's Chicken & Stars Soup
Bowl of fresh spinach leaves garnished with juicy tomato
  wedges, crunchy chopped celery, sweet grated carrots and
  lemon wedge
3 crisp onion-flavored breadsticks (5″ long × ½″ diameter each)
"Coconut Milk" (1 cup frosty cold skim milk with ¼ teaspoon
  coconut extract)

SNACK
1 cup prepared Campbell's Crispy Spanish Style Vegetable
  Soup
1 serving Herbed Croutons*

DINNER
3 ounces tender lean roast beef
1 Stuffed Baked Potato*
Thin crisp cucumber slices mixed with sliced red radishes and
  sprinkled with wine vinegar
½ cup chilled unsweetened cherries
Steaming hot coffee or tea

SNACK
1 cup prepared Campbell's Turkey Noodle Soup
Chilled lightly steamed fresh or frozen broccoli flowerets sprinkled with lemon juice

Day 7

BRUNCH

½ cup fresh juicy unsweetened orange slices tossed with ½ cup
 fresh watercress
1 serving Crustless Mixed Vegetable Quiche*
1 small warmed dinner roll
Bubbly cold mineral water with slice of fresh lime
Steaming hot coffee or tea

SNACK

1 cup prepared Campbell's Beef Broth Soup
Platter of fresh crunchy raw vegetables
1 serving Cucumber Yogurt Dip*

DINNER

1 cup prepared Campbell's Chicken Gumbo Soup
2 ounces fresh grilled salmon
½ cup hot and fluffy brown rice cooked with basil
1 serving Spicy Green Bean Salad*
1 serving Mixed Fruit Sherbet*

SNACK

1 cup prepared Campbell's Consommé (Beef) Soup
3 crisp rye wafers

*Crustless Mixed Vegetable Quiche, Citrus/Watercress Salad, Rolls
& Mineral Water*

Day 8

BREAKFAST OR MIDMORNING SNACK
2 chilled medium unsweetened plums
½ crunchy toasted bagel or English muffin
Steaming hot coffee or tea

LUNCH
1 cup prepared Campbell's Crispy Spanish Style Vegetable Soup
2 ounces thin-sliced tender roast beef on seeded kaiser roll with crisp fresh lettuce and tomato and onion slices and 1 teaspoon mustard
1 cup frosty cold skim milk

SNACK
1 cup prepared Campbell's Turkey Noodle Soup
Crisp zucchini fingers

DINNER
1 cup prepared Campbell's Chicken Gumbo Soup
1 fresh egg scrambled in nonstick skillet with 1 slice reduced-fat process cheese and lightly steamed chopped scallions and mushrooms
1 fresh tomato (with top sliced off) grilled with basil
Chilled chopped cucumber and celery salad sprinkled with fresh lime juice
Café au Lait (1 cup steaming hot coffee mixed with 1 cup warmed skim milk)

SNACK
1 warm baked unsweetened small apple with cinnamon topped with 1 serving Whipped Topping*

Day 9

BREAKFAST OR MIDMORNING SNACK
1 chilled juicy small orange, cut into wedges
1 slice cheesy rye toast (1 slice reduced-fat process cheese
    melted over 1 slice freshly toasted rye bread)
Steaming hot coffee or tea

LUNCH
1 cup prepared Campbell's Chicken Noodle Soup
1 serving Marinated Vegetable Mélange*
3 crunchy melba toast rounds
Frosty Vanilla Cooler (1 cup frosty cold skim milk mixed with
    1 teaspoon vanilla extract)

SNACK
1 cup prepared Campbell's Consommé (Beef) Soup
1 serving Herbed Croutons*

DINNER
1 cup prepared Campbell's Won Ton Soup
1 serving Deviled Oven-Fried Chicken*
Steamed fresh green beans with dash of ground marjoram
Tangy Lemon and Lime Yogurt (1/2 cup lowfat yogurt mixed
    with 1/2 teaspoon fresh lemon juice and 1/2 teaspoon fresh
    lime juice)

SNACK
2 chilled juicy unsweetened peach halves

Day 10

BREAKFAST OR MIDMORNING SNACK
2 medium chilled unsweetened pear halves
1 slice crisp whole wheat toast
1½ cups frosty cold skim milk
Steaming hot coffee or tea

LUNCH
1 cup prepared Campbell's Chicken Gumbo Soup
Soft Chicken Taco (1 steamed corn tortilla wrapped around
    filling of 1 ounce shredded hot chicken with 1 teaspoon
    chopped onion, 2 tablespoons chopped tomatoes and ¼ cup
    shredded lettuce seasoned with fresh lime juice)
Mexican Salad of chopped sweet green peppers, juicy toma-
    toes, crunchy celery and zucchini sprinkled with wine vine-
    gar
Lemony Iced Tea

SNACK
1 cup prepared Campbell's Won Ton Soup
Crunchy carrot sticks

DINNER
3 ounces lemon broiled fresh trout
1 serving Summer Squash au Gratin*
Crisp tossed salad of crunchy romaine lettuce and red radishes
    with fresh lemon wedge
1 serving Frozen Blueberry Yogurt Delight*
Steaming hot coffee or tea

SNACK
1 cup prepared Campbell's Chicken Noodle Soup
2 slices crisp thin flatbread wafers

KICK-OFF DIET RECIPES

Vegetable Scramble

2 tablespoons water
1 cup chopped fresh tomato (1 medium)
¹/₂ cup chopped celery
¹/₂ cup chopped green pepper
¹/₄ cup chopped onion
¹/₂ teaspoon basil leaves, crushed
¹/₄ teaspoon salt
¹/₈ teaspoon pepper
4 eggs
4 teaspoons water

In 10-inch nonstick skillet, in 2 tablespoons water, cook tomato, celery, green pepper and onion with basil, salt and pepper until tender.

Meanwhile, in small bowl, beat eggs and 4 teaspoons water; pour into skillet. Cook over low heat. As mixture begins to set around edges, gently lift cooked portions with turner so that thin, uncooked portion can flow to bottom. Continue gently lifting cooked portions until eggs are set, but still moist. Makes 4 servings.

Fruit Crème

¹/₂ small ripe banana or 1 medium peach
¹/₂ cup evaporated skim milk
Dash ground nutmeg
1 ice cube

In electric blender, combine all ingredients; cover. Blend on high speed until smooth. Pour into glass. Makes 1 serving (1 cup).

Herbed Croutons

2 slices whole wheat bread
$^{1}/_{4}$ teaspoon basil leaves, crushed
$^{1}/_{4}$ teaspoon oregano leaves, crushed
$^{1}/_{8}$ teaspoon garlic powder

Cut bread into $^{1}/_{2}$-inch cubes; spread in single layer on baking sheet. Mix basil, oregano and garlic powder; sprinkle on croutons. Bake at 300°F. for 25 minutes or until browned; stir often. Makes 4 servings ($^{1}/_{3}$ cup each).

Marvelous Manicotti

8 manicotti macaroni ($^{1}/_{4}$ pound)
1 can (10$^{3}/_{4}$ ounces) condensed tomato soup
$^{1}/_{2}$ cup water
$^{1}/_{2}$ teaspoon basil leaves, crushed
1$^{1}/_{4}$ teaspoons oregano leaves, crushed
1 pound ground veal
1 cup chopped fresh mushrooms
1 medium green pepper, chopped (1 cup)
1 medium clove garlic, minced
$^{1}/_{8}$ teaspoon pepper

Cook manicotti in unsalted water following package directions; drain.

Meanwhile, to make sauce, in small saucepan, combine soup, water, basil and $^{1}/_{4}$ teaspoon oregano; cook over low heat 10 minutes. Stir often.

To make filling, in nonstick skillet or skillet sprayed with nonstick cooking spray, brown veal and mushrooms and cook green pepper with garlic, pepper and remaining 1 teaspoon oregano until tender. Stir to separate meat; add $^{1}/_{3}$ cup sauce.

Reserve 1 cup filling; fill manicotti with remaining filling. Arrange 4 filled manicotti in 1$^{1}/_{2}$-quart shallow baking dish ($10 \times 6 \times 2''$). Combine remaining sauce and reserved filling; spoon $^{1}/_{2}$ sauce mixture over manicotti.* Cover; bake at 350°F. for 30 minutes or until hot. Makes 4 servings.

---

*In 1$^{1}/_{2}$-quart shallow baking dish ($10 \times 6 \times 2''$), arrange remaining 4 filled manicotti. Spoon remaining sauce mixture over manicotti. Cover with freezer-proof wrap; freeze. To reheat, bake, covered, at 350°F. for 50 minutes or until hot. Makes 4 servings.

Individual Pita Pizzas

*¹/₂ can (10³/₄-ounce size) condensed tomato
   soup*
¹/₄ cup water
¹/₂ teaspoon oregano leaves, crushed
¹/₈ teaspoon garlic powder
*2 individual pita breads (sandwich pockets), 6
   inch*
*1 cup shredded part-skim mozzarella cheese
   (4 ounces)*

In small saucepan, combine soup, water, oregano and garlic;
cook over low heat 10 minutes. Stir often.

Meanwhile, split each pita bread into 2 circles; toast.
Spread each with 2 tablespoons soup mixture; sprinkle with ¼
cup cheese. Arrange on broiler pan. Broil 4 inches from heat 3
minutes or until cheese melts. Makes 4 servings.

Cucumber Yogurt Dip

¹/₂ cup plain lowfat yogurt
¹/₄ cup finely chopped cucumber
¹/₄ teaspoon tarragon leaves, crushed
¹/₄ teaspoon garlic powder
Dash crushed red pepper

In small bowl, combine all ingredients; chill. Serve as a dip
with fresh vegetables. Makes 1 serving (¾ cup).

Hawaiian Chicken Kabobs

1 can (8 ounces) apricots in juice
¹/₂ teaspoon ground ginger
¹/₄ teaspoon garlic powder
¹/₈ teaspoon crushed red pepper
*2 whole chicken breasts, skinned and boned
   (1 pound boneless), cut in 16 pieces*
1 medium green pepper, cut in squares
8 small whole fresh mushrooms

Drain apricots, reserving juice; quarter apricot halves.

To make marinade, in shallow dish, combine reserved juice, ginger, garlic and red pepper; add chicken. Toss well; chill 1 hour or more.

Meanwhile, in small saucepan, in 1 inch boiling water, cook green pepper 1 minute; drain. Remove chicken from marinade, reserving marinade.

On each of 4 skewers, arrange chicken, green pepper, mushrooms and apricots. Place on broiler pan. Broil 4 inches from heat 10 minutes or until done, turning often and brushing with marinade. Makes 4 servings.

Curried Cauliflower Polonaise

6 tablespoons fresh bread crumbs
2 teaspoons curry powder
2 hard-cooked eggs, chopped
2 tablespoons grated Parmesan cheese
1 tablespoon chopped fresh parsley
6 cups fresh or frozen cauliflowerets

In small nonstick skillet or skillet sprayed with nonstick cooking spray, over low heat, brown bread crumbs with curry powder. Stir often. Add eggs, cheese and parsley.

Meanwhile, in medium saucepan, in 1 inch boiling water, heat cauliflowerets to boiling. Reduce heat to low; cover. Simmer 5 minutes or until tender-crisp. Drain. Sprinkle with bread crumb mixture. Makes 4 servings (1½ cups each).

Rice Stuffed Tomatoes

½ can (10½-ounce size) condensed
    consommé
¾ cup water
½ cup raw regular long-grain rice
1 small clove garlic, minced
¼ teaspoon dried dill weed or 1 teaspoon
    chopped fresh dill
⅛ teaspoon pepper
4 medium tomatoes
Salad greens

In small saucepan, combine all ingredients except tomatoes and greens. Cover; bring to boil. Reduce heat to low; cook 20 minutes or until liquid is absorbed. Stir occasionally. Chill.

Place tomatoes stem-end down. With knife, cut each tomato almost to stem end, making 6 sections; spread apart slightly.

Carefully cut out and chop enough tomato pulp to measure 1/2 cup; stir into rice. Place tomatoes on salad greens; fill with rice mixture. Garnish with fresh dill. Makes 4 servings.

Spiced Whole Wheat Pancakes

2/3 cup whole wheat flour
1 1/4 teaspoons baking powder
1 teaspoon ground cinnamon
1/2 teaspoon ground nutmeg
1/2 cup skim milk
1 egg, slightly beaten
4 teaspoons vegetable oil
1/4 cup water

To make batter, in bowl, combine flour, baking powder, cinnamon and nutmeg. Add remaining ingredients. Stir until flour is just moistened.

Preheat a nonstick griddle or griddle sprayed with nonstick cooking spray. Spoon 2 tablespoons batter for each pancake on hot griddle. Cook until golden brown on each side. Makes 4 servings (2 pancakes each).

Stuffed Baked Potatoes

4 small baking potatoes (1 pound)
1/2 cup skim milk
1/4 teaspoon salt
1/8 teaspoon pepper
Dash crushed thyme leaves
2 tablespoons finely chopped green onions
1/8 teaspoon paprika

Bake potatoes until done. With sharp knife, cut slice from top of each. Scoop out insides, leaving thin shell; reserve shells.

On medium speed of electric mixer, mash potatoes; gradually add milk, salt, pepper and thyme. Beat until light and fluffy. Stir in green onions. Spoon into reserved shells; sprinkle with paprika.

Place on broiler pan. Broil 4 inches from heat 5 minutes or until lightly browned. Makes 4 servings.

Crustless Mixed Vegetable Quiche

2¹/₂ cups frozen mixed vegetables (broccoli,
cauliflower and carrots)
4 eggs, slightly beaten
1 cup skim milk
4 ounces shredded reduced-fat process cheese
¹/₄ teaspoon ground nutmeg
¹/₈ teaspoon pepper

In medium saucepan, in 1 inch boiling water, bring vegetables to boil. Reduce heat to low; cover. Simmer 5 minutes or until tender-crisp; drain well.

In bowl, combine eggs, milk, ¹/₂ cup cheese, nutmeg and pepper; add vegetables.

Into 9″ pie plate or quiche pan sprayed with nonstick cooking spray, pour egg mixture; sprinkle with remaining cheese. Bake at 375°F. for 30 minutes or until knife inserted in center comes out clean. Makes 4 servings.

Spicy Green Bean Salad

1 pound fresh or frozen cut green beans (4
cups)
¹/₂ can (10³/₄-ounce size) condensed chicken
broth
1 tablespoon fresh lemon juice
1 teaspoon Worcestershire sauce
1 small clove garlic, minced
¹/₄ cup diced pimiento

In medium saucepan, in 1 inch boiling water, heat green beans to boiling. Reduce heat to low; cover. Simmer 5 minutes or until tender-crisp. Drain.

In shallow dish, combine broth, lemon juice, Worcestershire and garlic; add beans and pimiento. Toss well; chill. Makes 4 servings (1 cup each).

Mixed Fruit Sherbet

---

*2 packages (10 ounces each) frozen
    unsweetened mixed fruits, thawed (4 cups
    total)
¹/₂ teaspoon unflavored gelatin
³/₄ cup skim milk
1 teaspoon vanilla extract*

Drain fruit, reserving ¹/₄ cup juice.

In small saucepan, sprinkle gelatin over reserved juice to soften. Place over low heat, stirring until gelatin is dissolved.

Pour into electric blender; add fruit, milk and vanilla. Cover; blend on high speed until smooth. Pour into bowl.

Cover; freeze until firm, stirring occasionally. On medium speed of electric mixer, beat until smooth but still frozen. Freeze until firm.

Let stand at room temperature 10 minutes before serving. Makes 8 servings (¹/₂ cup each).

Whipped Topping

---

*¹/₂ cup cold water
¹/₄ cup instant nonfat dry milk
1 teaspoon unflavored gelatin
1 teaspoon fresh lemon juice
2 teaspoons vanilla extract*

In small saucepan, combine water and dry milk; sprinkle gelatin over mixture. Place over low heat, stirring until gelatin dissolves. Pour into small bowl; add lemon juice and vanilla. Chill until slightly thickened.

On high speed of electric mixer, beat gelatin mixture until soft peaks form (about 5 minutes). Serve immediately.* Makes 4 servings (¹/₂ cup each).

---

*Beat leftover topping with electric mixer until fluffy (yield will be less).

Marinated Vegetable Mélange

2 cups fresh or frozen small broccoli flowerets
2 cups fresh or frozen small cauliflowerets
1 cup chopped carrots
1/2 can (10 1/2-ounce size) condensed beef broth
1 tablespoon tarragon vinegar
2 small cloves garlic, minced
1 teaspoon Italian seasoning, crushed

In medium saucepan, in 1 inch boiling water, heat vegetables to boiling. Reduce heat to low; cover. Simmer 3 minutes or until tender-crisp; drain.

In shallow dish, combine remaining ingredients; add vegetables. Toss well; chill. Makes 4 servings (3/4 cup each).

Deviled Oven-Fried Chicken

1 tablespoon dry mustard
2 tablespoons water
1/4 teaspoon Worcestershire sauce
1/2 cup fresh bread crumbs
1 teaspoon paprika
1/8 teaspoon garlic powder
2 whole chicken breasts, split, skinned and
    boned (1 pound boneless)

Combine mustard, water and Worcestershire; let stand a few minutes.

In shallow dish, combine bread crumbs, paprika and garlic powder. Brush chicken evenly with mustard mixture; dip in bread crumb mixture.

Arrange in 1 1/2-quart shallow baking dish (10 × 6 × 2"); sprinkle with additional paprika. Bake at 400°F. for 20 minutes or until done. Makes 4 servings.

Summer Squash au Gratin

1/4 cup seasoned fine dry bread crumbs
4 teaspoons grated Parmesan cheese
1/2 can (10 3/4-ounce size) condensed tomato
soup
2 tablespoons water
1/4 cup chopped onion
1 small clove garlic, minced
1 teaspoon basil leaves, crushed
1/8 teaspoon pepper
3/4 pound zucchini squash (2 small), cut in
1/4-inch slices
3/4 pound yellow summer squash (2 small), cut
in 1/4-inch slices

In small nonstick skillet or skillet sprayed with nonstick cooking spray, combine bread crumbs and cheese. Brown over low heat; stir often.

In small saucepan, combine soup, water, onion, garlic, basil and pepper. Cover; cook over low heat 10 minutes. Stir often.

Meanwhile, in medium saucepan, in 1 inch boiling water, combine zucchini and yellow squash. Heat to boiling; reduce heat to low. Cover; simmer 5 minutes or until tender-crisp. Drain. Add soup mixture; heat. Garnish with bread crumb mixture. Makes 4 servings (1 1/2 cups each).

Frozen Blueberry Yogurt Delight

2 cups fresh or frozen unsweetened
blueberries, thawed (8 ounces)
1 cup plain lowfat yogurt
1 teaspoon vanilla extract
1/8 teaspoon ground nutmeg

In electric blender, combine all ingredients; cover. Blend on high speed until smooth; pour into bowl.

Cover; freeze until firm. On medium speed of electric mixer, beat until smooth but still frozen. Freeze until firm.

Let stand at room temperature 10 minutes before serving. Makes 4 servings (1/2 cup each).

INTRODUCTION TO THE SOUP DIET FOOD GROUPS
. . . a practical food guide for weight control

No doubt you've heard that variety is the spice of life. But do you know it's also the secret to a balanced diet? Foods differ in types and amounts of nutrients, and no single food provides all the essential nutrients in the correct amounts needed for optimum health. Therefore, it is important to eat variety of foods daily. But sometimes, particularly if you are dieting, you need help to make sure you are getting the foods you need.

The Soup Diet helps assure the correct amount and variety of foods each day by combining human nutrient needs and the nutritive values of foods into a simple selection guide. Using ten groups of foods sorted by similar nutritional content, the Soup Diet takes the dreariness out of controlling your weight by allowing you to choose whole groups of foods, rather than tediously counting calories, carbohydrates, fats or other nutrients. The Soup Diet is just what you need to simplify your weight-control efforts.

SO HOW DOES IT WORK?

The Soup Diet Food Groups contain measured amounts of everyday foods you can find at your supermarket. Since the individual groups contain foods of similar nutrient and caloric value, foods in one group can be "traded" with other foods in the same group. For instance, you can trade a peach for a pear or a bowl of oatmeal for a slice of bread. It's very simple, and the combinations are endless. You will find it flexible enough to prevent "diet boredom."

The Soup Diet Take-It-Off and Keep-It-Off-Forever Plans both use the Soup Diet Food Groups. The Soup Diet Food Groups are:

- Dairy Delights (milk, yogurt)
- Filler Foods
  —Ad Lib Veggies (vegetables you can eat as much of as desired)
  —Limited Veggies (vegetables for which portion servings are specified)
- Nature's Treats (fruits, fruit juices)
- Complex Carbs (breads, cereals, pastas and starchy vegetables)

- Protein Providers (meats, fish, poultry, cheese, meat substitutes)
- Palate Pleasers (margarine, oils, salad dressings and other fats)
- The Soup Group
- Flexi-Foods
- Freebies
- Fling Foods

The Soup Diet Take-It-Off and Keep-It-Off-Forever Plans take into account the number of calories that are right for you, depending on your sex and whether you wish to reduce or maintain your weight. They recommend the total daily servings from each Soup Diet Food Group.

Those servings should be divided each day into at least three meals or a combination of meals and sensible snacks. You are free to design your own menus, but you must include the daily total servings from each group as prescribed by the Soup Diet plan you are following. For example, if your plan calls for 2 servings of Dairy Delights, your menus should contain 2 cups skim or lowfat milk or 1 cup skim or lowfat milk and ½ cup skim or lowfat yogurt or any such combination of foods in the serving sizes listed in Dairy Delights on page 81.

Your body needs refueling at regular intervals so it is important to eat at least three meals a day. Realize that a meal doesn't always mean a lot of food. You may prefer to eat 2 or 3 light meals plus snacks. It is the *total* intake, well spaced, that matters.

HOW TO FOLLOW THE SOUP DIET PLANS

The first step is to familiarize yourself with which foods belong in each group. Then determine the Soup Diet plan you need, and study the sample menus of that plan to see how your food group allowances can be translated into delicious and convenient meals.

The next step is to plan your own menus. Planning menus can safeguard you from diet failure. By planning ahead, you have the foods your plan recommends when you need them. Use only foods listed in the food groups. Be sure to include the total servings from each Soup Diet Food Group as prescribed by the plan you are following. Also remember to plan at least 3 meals (or meals plus snacks) per day. Plan menus in advance; make them suit your taste and life-style.

Continue to use food records as instructed in Chapter II. Write down daily the foods you eat, identify their food groups and portion sizes and keep totals for each day. This will help you remain aware of the amount of food you eat and continue to enlighten you about your eating habits.

WHAT ABOUT FOODS NOT IN THE SOUP DIET FOOD GROUPS?

You will notice that some foods like potato chips and ice cream and French fries are not listed in The Soup Diet Food Groups that follow. Some of these foods may be added back to your diet, in moderation of course, in the Keep-It-Off-Forever Plan. Once you reach your ideal weight and move on to the Keep-It-Off Plan, you'll find such foods listed in Fling Foods. Because of their limited nutritional value, or high content of sugar or fat, these foods are omitted from the low-calorie Take-It-Off Plan. With any low-calorie diet, you should include foods rich in nutrients while low in calories.

SOUP AND THE SOUP DIET TAKE-IT-OFF AND KEEP-IT-OFF-FOREVER PLANS

Obviously, soup is a very important part of the Soup Diet Take-It-Off and Keep-It-Off-Forever Plans. By slowing your eating pace, soup can limit the urge to overeat. Soup is easy to include in most life-styles, and flavor varieties can please just about everyone. Just let the Soup Diet work for you.

THE SOUP DIET FOOD GROUPS

DAIRY DELIGHTS

Dairy foods are an important part of the Soup Diet. The major source of calcium in any diet, dairy foods as listed below also provide protein, phosphorous, B-complex vitamins and Vitamins A and D. A well-balanced diet includes 2 servings of these foods daily.

Both the Take-It-Off Plan and the Keep-It-Off-Forever Plan call for 2 servings of Dairy Delights every day. Drink milk with meals or as a snack or an addition to cereal, coffee or tea. You do not have to drink skim milk if you do not care for it. But if you drink lowfat milk, you must eat less of the Palate Pleasers than your plan allows. For example, if your plan gives you 4 Palate Pleasers for the whole day and you drink 1 cup of lowfat milk, you must subtract 1 Palate Pleaser leaving your total for the day 3 Palate Pleasers.

If you don't like to drink milk, you will find several recipes in both the Take-It-Off Plan and the Keep-It-Off-Forever Plan that can make getting your daily Dairy Delights easy.

CHOICES	SERVING SIZE
Skim or nonfat milk	1 cup
Lowfat (1 percent or 2 percent milk; subtract 1 Palate Pleaser)	1 cup
Powdered (nonfat dry, before adding liquid)	$1/3$ cup
Canned, evaporated skim milk, undiluted	$1/2$ cup
Canned, evaporated lowfat milk, undiluted (subtract 1 Palate Pleaser)	$1/2$ cup
Yogurt, plain, unflavored, made from skim or lowfat milk	$1/2$ cup

FILLER FOODS

Besides contributing to sound nutritional health, Filler Foods can help you feel full while trying to lose weight. Even when you're not dieting, vegetables are a great way to eat a lot yet keep your weight down.

Since individual vegetables differ in the nutrients they contribute to the diet, you should eat a variety. Dark green and deep yellow vegetables are good sources of Vitamin A. Vegetables are an important source of fiber, and if not overcooked, most green vegetables are reliable sources of Vitamin C. Some vegetables are good sources of potassium while others provide moderate amounts of the B-complex vitamins.

Use fresh or frozen vegetables, eaten raw or cooked, prepared without sauce or fat unless as specified in the Soup Diet recipes. Avoid batter-fried vegetables. To prevent nutrient losses, vegetables should be steamed or cooked in small amounts of water for short periods of time. Because the calorie content of vegetables varies, some vegetables can be eaten in amounts as desired, while others should be limited to ½ cup daily. When selecting vegetables for the day, be sure to include at least one that is a good source of Vitamin A.

AD LIB VEGGIES

Eat at least 2 servings of 2 different vegetables each day. One serving equals ½ cup or 1 medium vegetable (such as 1 medium tomato).

CHOICES

Asparagus**
Beans, green or yellow
Bean sprouts
Broccoli***
Brussels sprouts***
Cabbage*
Carrots**
Cauliflower*
Celery
Chinese cabbage
Cucumbers
Eggplant
Endive**
Greens:
  Beet**
  Chard
  Chicory

Collards*
Dandelion**
Escarole
Kale***
Lettuce
Mustard***
Spinach***
Turnip***
Mushrooms
Parsley***
Peppers, green or red*
Radishes
Squash, summer
Turnips*
Tomatoes***
Watercress***
Zucchini

LIMITED VEGGIES—Optional

Because of their higher carbohydrate and calorie content, you should eat no more than ½ cup or 4 ounces total of these vegetables per day. Servings from this group daily are not required, but they do add variety and flavor to meals.

CHOICES

Artichoke and artichoke hearts	Parsnips
Beets	Peas, green**
Chinese pea pods (snow peas)	Pumpkin**
Jicama	Rutabagas
Leeks	Scallions
Okra	Shallots
Onions	Squash, winter***
	Water chestnuts

NATURE'S TREATS

Nature's Treats add variety and a satisfying sweet touch to snacks, salads, entrees and desserts. As an added bonus, Nature's Treats are also excellent sources of vitamins, minerals and fiber.

In choosing your daily Nature's Treats, be sure to select at least one that is a good source of Vitamin C. Some Nature's Treats such as bananas, apricots, grapefruit, grapefruit juice, oranges and orange juice also add significant amounts of potassium to the diet.

Nature's Treats may be used fresh, dried, frozen, canned in water or juice, or in juice form, providing no sugar has been added.

---

*Good source of Vitamin C
**Good source of Vitamin A
***Good source of Vitamins A and C

CHOICES	SERVING SIZE
Apple, fresh	1 small
juice	$1/3$ cup
Applesauce, unsweetened	$1/2$ cup
Apricots, fresh**	2 medium
canned**	4 halves
dried**	4 halves
Banana	$1/2$ small
Berries:	
blackberries	$1/2$ cup
blueberries	$1/2$ cup
raspberries	$1/2$ cup
strawberries*	$3/4$ cup
Cherries, fresh	10 large
canned	$1/2$ cup
Cranberry juice cocktail	$1/4$ cup
Dates	2
Figs, fresh or dried	1
Fruit cocktail or salad, fresh, frozen or canned, juice or water packed	$1/2$ cup
Grapefruit, fresh*	$1/2$ medium
juice*	$1/2$ cup
sections*	$1/2$ cup
Grapes, fresh	12 medium
juice	$1/4$ cup
Kiwi*	1 medium
Mango***	$1/2$ small
Melon	
cantaloupe***	$1/4$ small or $1/2$ cup
honeydew*	$1/8$ medium or $1/2$ cup
watermelon	1 cup

---

*Good source of Vitamin C
**Good source of Vitamin A
***Good source of Vitamins A and C

CHOICES	SERVING SIZE
Nectarine**	1 medium
Orange, fresh*	1 small
juice*	1/2 cup
sections*	1/2 cup
Papaya***	1/2 cup
Peach, fresh**	1 medium
canned**	1/2 cup or 2 medium halves
Pear, fresh	1 small
canned	2 small halves
Persimmon**	1 medium
Pineapple, fresh or canned, packed in own juice, all styles	1/2 cup or 2 slices
juice	1/3 cup
Plums, fresh	2 medium
canned	2 whole
Prunes, dried	2 medium
Raisins	2 tablespoons
Tangerine*	1 medium

COMPLEX CARBS

Complex Carbs include whole-grain or enriched breads, cereals and pastas and starchy vegetables. This group is an important source of B-complex vitamins and iron and also provides protein and other essential vitamins, minerals and fiber. Whole-grain products have more fiber than products made from refined flours. Starchy vegetables are included in this group, because they provide a similar amount of carbohydrate as one serving of bread.

Prepare cooked cereals, rice and other grains, pastas and popcorn without salt.

CHOICES	SERVING SIZE
Breads	
Bread (white, French or Italian, whole wheat, rye, pumpernickel or raisin)	1 slice
Bagel, small	1/2
Biscuit, small (subtract 1 Palate Pleaser)	1
Corn bread, 2-inch cube (subtract 1 Palate Pleaser)	1 cube
Corn muffin, small or "toaster" style (subtract 1 Palate Pleaser)	1
English muffin, small	1/2
Roll, dinner, 2- to 3-inch diameter	1
Frankfurter roll	1/2
Hamburger bun	1/2
Pancake or waffle, 5-inch diameter (subtract 1 Palate Pleaser)	1
Tortilla, corn, 6-inch	1
Pita bread	1/2 small
Cereals and Pasta	
Bran, buds or shredded	1/3 cup
Cold cereal, unsweetened, flakes or puffed	3/4 cup
Hot cereal, cooked	1/2 cup
Hot cereal, uncooked	1/4 cup
Rice, grits, hominy, barley, buckwheat groats, bulgur or wheat, cooked	1/2 cup
Spaghetti, noodles or macaroni, cooked	1/2 cup
Popcorn, air-popped, no added fat	2 cups
Wheat germ	1/4 cup

CHOICES   SERVING SIZE

Crackers
Arrowroot   3

Breadsticks, 5 inches long, 1/2-inch diameter   3

Flatbread, thin wafers   4

Graham, 2 1/2 inches square   2 squares

Matzo, 4 × 6 inches   1/2

Melba toast, rectangular slices   4
    rounds   6

Oysters   20

Rye wafers, 2 × 3 1/2 inches   3

Saltines   6

Legumes
Dry beans, peas, chick peas (garbanzos),
cooked   1/2 cup

Baked beans, no pork, canned   1/4 cup

High-Carb Vegetables
Corn, whole kernel or cream style   1/3 cup

Corn on cob   1 small

Lima beans   1/2 cup

Mixed vegetables with corn and lima beans   1/2 cup

Potato, white, whole or mashed   1 small

Yam or sweet potato   1/4 cup

Prepared Ingredients
Cornmeal, dry   2 tablespoons

Dry bread crumbs   3 tablespoons

Flour or cornstarch   2 tablespoons

Tapioca   2 tablespoons

PROTEIN PROVIDERS

Besides being good sources of protein, many Protein Providers contribute iron, phosphorous and important B-complex vitamins to your diet. It is a good idea to vary your choices of Protein Providers as each has distinct nutritional advantages.

To keep your fat and cholesterol intake moderate, primarily choose chicken, turkey, fish and veal. Eat beef, pork, lamb, duck and goose no more than 3 times per week. Eat no more than 3 whole eggs per week. Limit cheese to no more than 4 servings per week. Foods should be boiled, broiled or roasted rather than fried. Trim all visible fat from meat and remove skin from poultry. Since peanut butter is high in fat, if you choose it subtract the correct number of Palate Pleasers from your daily total.

Dried beans, peas and other legumes are also Protein Providers. But if you choose these foods as your Protein Provider, include another Protein Provider such as an egg or a Dairy Delight or a Complex Carb such as whole wheat bread to add vital protein components missing from beans, peas and other legumes. These foods can also be used as Complex Carbs, so you will see them listed there, too.

The following serving sizes are based on weight after cooking.

CHOICES	SERVING SIZE
Cheeses	
Cheddar, Swiss, Muenster and mozzarella (subtract 1 Palate Pleaser)	1 ounce
Cottage, dry curd	½ cup
Cottage, lowfat	¼ cup
Farmer's	¼ cup
Ricotta (part skim)	¼ cup
Reduced-fat process	1 ounce
Parmesan	3 tablespoons
Egg, large, whole	1
whites only	2

CHOICES	SERVING SIZE
Fish and seafood	
Any fresh or frozen	1 ounce (4 × 2 × ¼ inch)
Canned salmon, tuna, mackerel, crab or lobster, water pack	1 ounce
Clams, oysters, scallops, shrimp	5 small or 3 medium
Sardines, drained	3
Meat and poultry	
Beef, lamb, pork, veal, liver, chicken	1 ounce (1 ounce slice = 4 × 2 × ¼ inch)
Canned chicken, loosely packed	¼ cup
Meat substitutes	
Dry beans, peas, chick peas (garbanzos), other legumes	¼ cup
Peanut butter (subtract 2 Palate Pleasers)	2 tablespoons

Examples of 3-ounce servings (3 Protein Providers):
  —half a breast or leg and thigh of 2½- to 3-pound chicken
    —3 slices roast beef or pot roast, 4 × 2 × ¼ inch each
    —1 medium loin pork chop, ½ inch thick
    —1 hamburger patty, 3-inch diameter, ½ inch thick

PALATE PLEASERS

Palate Pleasers are important for satisfying meals. Acting not only as a carrier of flavors, Palate Pleasers can help you feel fuller longer. Palate Pleasers also provide essential fatty acids, elements required in your diet for good health.

To the dieter, Palate Pleasers have one major drawback. They're high in calories. So it is important to carefully control the amounts of Palate Pleasers used. If you can't judge accurately, measure!

Palate Pleasers come from both animal and plant sources, plants being the preferred source. Select liquid oils rather than solid shortenings. Use margarines that contain corn, safflower or sunflower oil listed as the first ingredient.

CHOICES	SERVING SIZE
Avocado, 4-inch diameter	$1/8$
Margarine, tub or stick or squeeze	1 teaspoon
diet	2 teaspoons
Dressing, French or Italian	1 tablespoon
Mayonnaise or salad dressing	2 teaspoons
Mayonnaise, reduced-calorie	1 tablespoon
Nuts:	
Almonds, whole	10
sliced	3 tablespoons
Pecans	4 halves
Peanuts	
Spanish	20 whole
Virginia	10 whole
Walnuts	6 small or 12 halves
Other	6 small
Oil	1 teaspoon
Seeds, pumpkin, sesame or sunflower	1 tablespoon

THE SOUP GROUP

By slowing the "dietary pace," soup can help you break the overeating habit. Soup is a quick and easy addition to a meal and can fit into everyone's eating style. Select a soup according to the Soup Diet plan you are following. To add variety, mix soups. For example, tomato soup mixed with cream of mushroom soup makes a tasty new dish.

Soups should be reconstituted with water. If milk is used, count it as a serving from Dairy Delights.

Take-It-Off Plan Soup Group
    Select two 1-cup servings of prepared Campbell's Soup per day.

Beef broth (bouillon) soup
Beef noodle soup
Beef with vegetables and barley soup
Beefy mushroom soup
Black bean soup
Chicken alphabet soup
Chicken 'n dumplings soup
Chicken & stars soup
Chicken broth soup
Chicken broth and rice soup
Chicken broth and vegetables soup
Chicken gumbo soup
Chicken barley soup
Chicken noodleO's soup
Chicken noodle soup
Chicken vegetable soup
Chicken with rice soup
Chunky vegetable soup
Clam chowder (Manhattan style)
Clam chowder (New England style)
Consommé (beef) soup
Cream of asparagus soup
Cream of celery soup
Cream of chicken soup
Cream of mushroom soup
Cream of onion soup
Cream of potato soup
Cream of shrimp soup
Cream of vegetable soup
Crispy Spanish style vegetable (gazpacho) soup
Crispy tomato garden soup
Curly noodle with chicken soup
French onion soup
Golden mushroom soup
Minestrone soup
Mushroom barley soup
Noodles & ground beef soup
Old fashioned vegetable soup
Oyster stew soup

Pepper pot soup
Scotch broth soup
Tomato soup
Turkey noodle soup
Turkey vegetable soup
Vegetable beef soup
Vegetable soup
Vegetarian vegetable soup
Won ton soup

Keep-It-Off-Forever Plan Soup Group

Select one 1-cup serving of prepared Campbell's Soup per day. On the Keep-It-Off-Forever Plan you can select from both Take-It-Off and Keep-It-Off-Forever Plan Soup Groups.

Bean with bacon soup
Cheddar cheese soup
Chili beef soup
Chunky steak and potato soup
Chunky turkey soup
Chunky beef soup
Chunky beef with noodles soup
Chunky chicken soup
Chunky chicken with rice soup
Chunky chicken vegetable soup
Chunky chili beef soup
Chunky clam chowder (Manhattan style)
Chunky Mediterranean vegetable soup
Chunky mexicali bean soup
Chunky minestrone soup
Chunky old fashioned bean with ham soup
Chunky old fashioned vegetable beef soup
Chunky sirloin burger soup
Chunky split pea with ham soup
Creamy chicken mushroom soup
Green pea soup
Meatball alphabet soup
Old fashioned tomato rice soup
"Soup for One" Old fashioned bean with ham soup
"Soup for One" Burly vegetable beef soup
"Soup for One" New England clam chowder
"Soup for One" Full flavored chicken vegetable soup
"Soup for One" Golden chicken & noodles soup

"Soup for One" Savory cream of mushroom soup
"Soup for One" Tomato royale soup
"Soup for One" Old world vegetable soup
Split pea with ham and bacon soup
Tomato bisque soup

FLEXI-FOODS

Flexi-Foods give you a way to add extra flavor to meals without adding too many extra calories. Soups in condensed form for use in recipes are included. The amount listed (1/8 can) is what you get per serving when you use 1/2 of 10 1/2 - to 11-ounce can of soup in a recipe that makes 4 servings.

There are two divisions within the Flexi-Foods group. You can choose 1 serving from each division daily if desired.

Division I—Choose 1 serving daily if desired

CHOICES	SERVING SIZE
Cocoa powder, unsweetened	1 tablespoon
Honey	1 tablespoon
Jelly, jam or preserves	1 tablespoon
Sugar, all kinds	1 tablespoon
Syrup, maple or other flavors	1 tablespoon
Tomato paste	2 tablespoons

Division II—Choose 1 serving daily if desired

CHOICES	SERVING SIZE
Campbell's Condensed Soups, undiluted (for use in cooking)	1/8 can (approximately 3 tablespoons)
Catsup	1 tablespoon
Chili sauce	1 tablespoon
Clam juice	1/4 cup
Tomato juice	1/3 cup
Tomato purée	1/4 cup
Tomato sauce	3 tablespoons
"V-8" Cocktail Vegetable Juice	1/3 cup

FREEBIES

You can use these foods freely when planning your meals and snacks.

Aromatic bitters
Club soda
Coffee
Cranberries, unsweetened
Mineral water
Rhubarb, unsweetened
Tea
Unflavored gelatin

You are allowed 1 choice of these for free each day.

Horseradish	1 tablespoon
Mustard, prepared	1 teaspoon
Worcestershire sauce	1 teaspoon

Seasonings can also be used freely. Consider these when preparing your next meal.

Allspice	Nutmeg
Basil	Seeds:
Bay leaves	Caraway
Chives	Celery
Chili powder	Dill
Cinnamon	Mustard
Cloves	Poppy
Curry powder	Onion powder
Dill	Oregano
Flavor extracts	Paprika
Garlic	Parsley
Ginger	Pepper
Lemon	Rosemary
Lemon pepper	Sage
Lime	Savory
Marjoram	Tarragon
Mint	Thyme
Mustard, dry	Vinegar

THE SOUP DIET TAKE-IT-OFF PLAN

The Soup Diet Take-It-Off Plan is a carefully developed weight-reduction plan designed to allow you to lose approximately 1 to 2 pounds a week. The 1200-calorie plan is suggested for women wishing to reduce. The 1500-calorie plan is designed for men. The 1500-calorie plan follows the 1200-calorie plan but simply allows additional servings of the Soup Diet Food Groups.

This plan allows you to reduce safely by moderately increasing fruits, vegetables, complex carbohydrates and fiber in the diet while modifying total sodium, sugar, fat and cholesterol. To assure you of getting enough vitamins and minerals at this low-calorie level, take a vitamin and mineral supplement daily. Women should look for a supplement with iron.

You can follow the Soup Diet Take-It-Off Plan as long as you need in order to reach your ideal weight. Once you and your doctor decide you have reached your goal, go on to the Soup Diet Keep-It-Off-Forever Plan.

Following is the Soup Diet Take-It-Off Daily Food Plan, which specifies the number of servings from each Food Group to eat daily. You do not have to carefully measure or weigh portions every time. However, if you cannot judge accurately, use a scale and cup measure for a couple of days until you learn to estimate correct portions.

The Soup Diet Take-It-Off Plan
1200 Calories*
Daily Food Plan

2 servings Dairy Delights	(see page 81)
Filler Foods:	(see page 81)
Ad Lib Veggies as desired	
1 serving Limited Veggies if desired	
3 servings Nature's Treats	(see page 83)
4 servings Complex Carbs**	(see page 85)
5 servings Protein Providers	(see page 88)
3 servings Palate Pleasers	(see page 89)
2 servings Flexi-Foods if desired	(see page 93)
2 servings Soup Group—Take-It-Off Group	(see page 91)

*This well-balanced diet is based on the U.S. Recommended Daily Allowances. Calories are derived about 50 percent from carbohydrate, 23 percent from protein and 27 percent from fat. However, to be sure you get enough vitamins and minerals at this low-calorie level, a vitamin and mineral supplement with iron is recommended daily.

**At least 1 serving must be an unsalted High-Carb Vegetable or cooked cereal, rice or other grain or pasta prepared without salt.

The Soup Diet Take-It-Off Plan
1500 Calories*
Daily Food Plan

2 servings Dairy Delights	(see page 81)
Filler Foods:	(see page 81)
Ad Lib Veggies as desired	
1 serving Limited Veggies if desired	
5 servings Nature's Treats	(see page 83)
5 servings Complex Carbs**	(see page 85)
6 servings Protein Providers	(see page 88)
4 servings Palate Pleasers	(see page 89)
2 servings Flexi-Foods if desired	(see page 93)
2 servings Soup Group—Take-It-Off Group	(see page 91)

*This well-balanced diet is based on the U.S. Recommended Daily Allowances. Calories are derived about 50 percent from carbohydrate, 23 percent from protein and 27 percent from fat. However, to be sure you get enough vitamins and minerals at this low-calorie level, a vitamin and mineral supplement is recommended daily.
**At least 2 servings must be an unsalted High-Carb Vegetable or cooked cereal, rice or other grain or pasta prepared without salt.

THE SOUP DIET KEEP-IT-OFF-FOREVER PLAN

Once you've achieved your desired weight and want to stay there, the Soup Diet Keep-It-Off Plan is all you need.

The Soup Diet Keep-It-Off Plan follows the same format as the Take-It-Off Plan but increases the total servings from the food groups and includes a special Fling Foods group. The plan continues to control the total sodium, sugar and fat in your diet.

Designed to add approximately 500 calories per day to stop your weight loss, the Keep-It-Off Plans range between 1700–2200 calories. The lower end of the range is generally for women, the higher end of the range for men. Depending on your individual needs and activities, decide which calorie level is best for you. Try starting out at the lower level, and if you continue to lose weight, move to the higher level. If you begin to gain weight, drop to a lower calorie level.

The additional servings from the Soup Diet Food Groups and the added Fling Foods make it easier to enjoy eating and still maintain your weight while at social events, traveling or dining out. The Soup Diet Keep-It-Off Plan gives you a guide to good eating you can follow the rest of your life.

The Soup Diet Keep-It-Off-Forever Plan
1700–2000–2200 Calories*
Daily Food Plan

1700 Calories	2000 Calories	2200 Calories	
2	2	3	servings Dairy Delights (see page 81)
			Filler Foods: (see page 81)
	Servings as desired		Ad Lib Veggies
1	2	3	servings Limited Veggies
4	6	8	servings Nature's Treats (see page 83)
7**	8**	9***	servings Complex Carbs (see page 85)
6	6	6	servings Protein Providers (see page 88)
6	7	9	servings Palate Pleasers (see page 89)
	2 servings if desired		servings Flexi-Foods (see page 93)
1	1	1	serving Soup Group (see page 91)

*This well-balanced diet is based on the U.S. Recommended Daily Allowances. Calories are derived 50-54 percent from carbohydrate, 19-21 percent from protein and 28-29 percent from fat.

**At least 3 servings must be an unsalted High-Carb Vegetable or cooked cereal, rice or other grain or pasta prepared without salt.

***At least 4 servings must be an unsalted High-Carb Vegetable, or cooked cereal, rice or other grain or pasta prepared without salt.

THE SOUP DIET KEEP-IT-OFF-FOREVER PLAN TIP SHEET

To help you successfully maintain your weight and enjoy eating, consider these guidelines:

• If you have been following the Soup Diet Take-It-Off Plan, continue to keep your food record for one month after you start the Keep-It-Off-Forever Plan. This acts as a safeguard to prevent regaining any weight as you gradually add foods to your eating plan.

- Check your weight daily, at the same time every day, using the same scale. Continue to use your weight graph.
- Set a five-pound weight-gain limit. If you exceed the limit, review and follow the lessons from Chapter II to bring your weight down again.
- Continue to eat at regular intervals. Skipping meals can trigger overeating.
- If you want to splurge on a vacation, prepare for it by losing weight *before* you go. "Eating today and dieting tomorrow" leads to weight gains.
- Continue to follow your exercise program.
- Reduce food intake sensibly at times when you are less active. If you cut down on activity but not food, you may be taking in more energy than you are expending.
- Get rid of clothes that are now too large, creating an obstacle to returning to your old weight (you won't have any clothes to wear).
- If you hit periods of stress in your life, don't try to lose weight. Just "aim to maintain."
- Care about yourself. Enjoy the new, slimmer you. Enjoy being what you wanted to be.
- Post the Soup Diet Keep-It-Off-Forever Plan in your kitchen for easy reference.

FLING FOODS

Certain foods have been limited in the Soup Diet. They may be of limited nutritional value or excessive in certain nutrients such as fat and sugar. However, for the special occasion or treat once you have reached your desired weight and are following the Keep-It-Off-Forever Plan, such foods can be worked into your diet. But should your weight start to climb, stop eating these foods until you're back down to your proper weight.

In general you need not be concerned about counting calories, but you should be aware of serving sizes and food group equivalents. Be aware that these foods are equal to other foods within the food groups named in calories only, *not* in nutritional value. They should not be used as the basis of your diet, just as a treat.

When faced with a restaurant or party menu, check this list to see how various foods can fit into your plan.

CHOICES	SERVING SIZE	APPROXIMATE FOOD GROUP EQUIVALENT
Alcoholic Beverages and Soda		
Beer	¾ cup (6 ounces)	1 Complex Carb
Gin, rum, whiskey, brandy and other liquors	1 fluid ounce	1 Complex Carb
Wine, sweet	2 fluid ounces	1 Complex Carb
Wine, dry	3 fluid ounces	1 Complex Carb
Ginger ale or cola	¾ cup (6 ounces)	1 Complex Carb
Fast Foods		
Pizza	½ of small pie (13-inch diameter)	7 Complex Carbs, 5 Protein Providers, 2 Palate Pleasers
Fish 'n chips	2-piece dinner	5 Complex Carbs, 2 Protein Providers, 9 Palate Pleasers
Fried chicken	3-piece dinner	4 Complex Carbs, 5 Protein Providers, 6 Palate Pleasers
Hamburger (1 meat patty, 1 bun)	1	2 Complex Carbs, 1½ Protein Providers, 1 Palate Pleaser
Hamburger (2 meat patties, 3 layers bread, dressing)	1	3 complex Carbs, 3 Protein Providers, 5 Palate Pleasers
Potatoes, French-fried, 2 to 3 inches long	8	1 Complex Carb, 1 Palate Pleaser
Potato or macaroni salad	½ cup	1 Complex Carb, 2 Palate Pleasers
Coleslaw	½ cup	2 Palate Pleasers
Snack Foods		
Potato or corn chips	15	1 Complex Carb, 2 Palate Pleasers
Pretzel sticks, 3⅛ inches long, ⅛-inch diameter	25	1 Complex Carb

CHOICES	SERVING SIZE	APPROXIMATE FOOD GROUP EQUIVALENT
Sweets		
Cake:		
Angel food	2 ½-inch wedge (2 ounces)	2 Complex Carbs
Cupcake, plain, without icing	1 3-inch	1 Complex Carb
Cookies:		
Gingersnaps	3 small	1 Complex Carb
Macaroons	2 medium	2 Complex Carbs 1 Palate Pleaser
Sugar wafers, 3½ × ½ inch	2	1 Complex Carb, ½ Palate Pleaser
Vanilla wafers	5 small	1 Complex Carb
Gelatin, fruit-flavored	¼ cup	1 Complex Carb
Ice Cream, vanilla, coffee, chocolate, strawberry, etc.	½ cup	1 Complex Carb 1 Palate Pleaser
Sherbet	½ cup	2 Complex Carbs
Yogurt, lowfat, frozen	½ cup or 1 bar	½ Complex Carb, ½ Protein Provider
Miscellaneous		
Coffee cream, light	2 tablespoons	1 Palate Pleaser
Sour cream	2 tablespoons	1 Palate Pleaser
Cream cheese	1 tablespoon	1 Palate Pleaser
Coconut, unsweetened (dried, shredded, flaked)	2 tablespoons	1 Palate Pleaser
Cream, heavy, whipped	1 tablespoon	1 Palate Pleaser

V

Making the Soup
Diet Work for You

Reading about a program and actually doing it are two different matters. Putting it into practice can be harder than you thought, especially if you have a family or a hectic schedule or some other consideration in your life. However, once you start the Soup Diet you should make a firm commitment to following the program and follow the instructions and suggestions as best you can. To simplify things as much as possible, this chapter tells you how to fit the Soup Diet to you, not you to it!

MODIFYING "BEHAVIOR MOD"

In Chapter II, Dr. Foreyt gave you a comprehensive program to change your eating habits. Those changes combined with a sensible eating program such as the Soup Diet can help you lose weight easily and keep it off. Following is a list of tips to make behavior modification fit even more easily into your life-style.

- Keeping food records can at first seem an awful chore. But after a short time, writing down the foods you eat will become second nature. To make it less of a chore, get in the habit of filling out your food record right before or right after you eat. If you develop this timing, you won't spend time trying to remember what you ate. That sometimes can be the most time-consuming part of keeping a food record.
- To prohibit you from doing *anything* while you eat so you can fully concentrate on eating might seem like a prescription for torture. But you can do a few other

things: enjoy your food, talk with your dinner partner, think pleasant thoughts of how good you'll look thin or listen to soft music. Concentrate on the positive instead of the negative. You soon won't miss television or other activities that used to take your mind away from the enjoyment of your food.

- If you find the "no seconds" rule almost too much to bear, try dividing your allotted portions in half, and eat only half at a time. Second servings of Ad Lib Veggies can help make the rule "easier to swallow."
- If your family insists on having serving plates at the table, keep the plates as far away from you as possible. You also might try to enlist their help in your weight-control efforts by explaining the reasons for keeping serving plates off the table.
- You can't always expect your family to eat only foods you are allowed. To lessen the temptation of foods that are there for your family to enjoy, put them in inaccessible places such as the back of the top shelf or in the freezer where you cannot easily get to them.
- If you find yourself constantly wanting to nibble, keep a supply of the Ad Lib Veggies cut up and ready for you in the refrigerator.

SURVIVAL AT THE GROCERY STORE

Planned, routinely timed trips to the grocery store and knowledge of the types of food to buy can make staying on the Soup Diet much easier. By following a few easy suggestions, you will have the foods you need readily available and be able to successfully avoid the temptations of "no-no's" that beckon to you from the grocery store shelves.

- *Plan menus in advance and make a shopping list.* It's much easier to stick to your diet when the food you need is readily available. By preparing menus for the week and making a shopping list, you will know the foods you need for that week and won't have to make extra trips to the grocery store. Also inventory the refrigerator, freezer and pantry before each shopping trip. A shopping list can also help you take advantage of newspaper ads and incorporate weekly specials into your menus. Saving money—an added bonus!

• *Comparison shop for calories.* Check the nutrition information panel on the label of many food products, and choose the ones with lower calorie counts. Pay special attention to the following:

—Always look for the lowest fat content in milk or cheese products.

—Look for lean cuts of meat. Higher-fat cuts often cost more and don't do much for your weight-control efforts.

—Play the substitution game. Look for calorie-cutting versions of fattening products. Experiment by using them in your favorite recipes. For example, evaporated skim milk can take the place of high-calorie cream in most sauces, casseroles, soufflés and desserts. It can even be whipped! Yogurt can take the place of sour cream, and low-calorie cream cheese has the same flavor as regular cream cheese.

—Diet margarine has half the calories of regular margarine, but it often can't replace regular margarine in recipes. Experiment first before you count on it in a recipe for a special meal.

—Check the diet section of the supermarket for fat-reduced products.

—Bottled flavor extracts from the supermarket's spice section are calorie bargains. Most spices and seasonings add so few calories to a dish that they need not be counted.

—Stay away from the "dietetic" product that does not list its calorie count. It may not be low in calories at all. For example, some "dietetic" candies made for diabetics have just as many calories as regular candy.

LOW-CALORIE COOKING—NUTRITIOUSLY

If you've never tried low-calorie cooking before, or if you're just looking for some pointers, try these:

—Use nonstick cooking sprays to help in no-fat cooking.

—Brown meat and poultry under the broiler instead of in a frying pan.

—Brown most lean meats and chicken in their own fat. Place meat in cold, nonstick skillet and add one tablespoon of water or other liquid. Cover and heat slowly. The liquid will evaporate, and the steam will cause the meat to release its own inner fat. Uncover the skillet, and let the meat brown in its own fat. Drain off any fat that accumulates before proceeding with your recipe.

—If time is at a premium, cook in double or triple quantities, then package the leftovers into homemade low-calorie frozen dinners.

—Enhance the flavor of foods with spices and herbs instead of sugars and fats. You can create some exciting new dishes from what you consider "plain ordinary fare" just by adding different spices or herbs.

—When reconstituting soups with milk, use skim milk to reduce total calories.

—Conserve nutrients while preparing foods;
  • Prepare raw or cooked vegetables close to serving time.
  • Wash produce quickly without soaking.
  • Keep chopping and peeling to a minimum.
  • Steam or cook vegetables with a small amount of water, tightly covered until just tender.
  • Save cooking liquids for sauces and soups.

HOW TO COPE WHEN DINING OUT

Your diet plan shouldn't turn you into an antisocial person. When you dine out, you can still eat well and continue to see pounds evaporate.

THE RESTAURANT

Chapter II gives very useful tips for dining out. Other pointers that are helpful in keeping to your diet include:

—Select restaurants that serve foods you can and should eat.

—Sometimes it may help to not even open the menu— order only what you know you should have.

—Be the first to order, so that foods chosen by others do not tempt you.

—Don't feel obligated to eat the whole serving. Leave as much as you can on your plate. You're not wasting money; you are saving calories.

—Double up on Ad Lib Veggies. When you order a salad, forget the dressing and season with lemon. Use pepper or other spices for extra flavor.

—Favor skim milk or club soda as your beverage in place of more fattening or stimulating drinks.

—Choose sourdough or whole-grain bread when available, and eat it plain without butter.

—Choose a fresh fruit salad or a piece of fresh fruit for dessert.

THE PARTY

Be totally open and frank about your new eating program with friends and relatives. While you cannot expect them to prepare special meals for you when you are invited to a dinner party, you can expect them to understand your right to eat in the manner you know is best for you. Most people are anxious to be helpful and will try to accommodate your needs.

To successfully conquer your own urges at a party, try these suggestions:

—When faced with a rich dessert, turn it down in favor of coffee. Avoid looking at the dessert. If you can't resist, ask for a small serving and eat only half.

—Survey that delectable buffet table of food before you dig in. Choose small amounts and foods low in calories and fats.

—If you find a bowl of peanuts at your elbow, move them or yourself.

THE TRAVELER

In the midst of a hectic traveling schedule, eating a healthful, well-balanced diet while maintaining your weight can be a challenge. If you're trying to lose weight, a nutritious diet may seem even farther out of reach.

Realize that if you are trying to lose weight you will have to be vigilant about your calorie needs and the calorie content of available foods. Also stay aware of the nutritional value of your meals: try to eat well-balanced meals three times a day. Before each trip, read through the tips for eating out on page 30.

As part of long-term weight maintenance, expect to gain a couple of pounds on a trip. So take off those pounds *before* your trip. That way you won't be faced with the added mental burden of knowing you *have* to lose to prevent your previous efforts from being wasted.

Following are tips for healthful low-calorie eating while traveling (or any time) and food choices that can give you more nutrition for your calories.

—Try to fit three meals a day into your schedule so you won't find yourself tempted to eat snacks that may not be of quality nutrition.

—Eat simply. Choose plain roasted, baked or broiled meats, fish and poultry. If you're eating out, order salad dressings, sauces and gravies to be served on the side.

—Opt for raw or lightly steamed vegetables to increase your vitamin and fiber intake.

—Make smart choices. If the only food available is from a vending machine, evaluate the choices for their nutrient content. Peanut butter and crackers give you more nutrition than a bag of corn chips.

—Go lightly on alcohol. Alcohol contains calories but none of the other vital nutrients needed in the diet. Too much alcohol may interfere with absorption and utilization of nutrients in the body.

—Carry an immersible heating coil and tea bags or packets of instant coffee so you can enjoy a pot of tea or coffee in your hotel room and avoid a trip to the vending machine area.

—Keep a thermos handy and ask the hotel kitchen to heat soup for you before you leave for the day. Then you'll have available a nutritious, filling food when you need it.

—Airlines offer special meals just for the asking. Just tell your travel or ticket agent the kind of meal you want.

VI

The Soup Diet
Sample Menus and
Recipes

Proving that dieting doesn't have to be complicated or boring, the easy-to-follow Soup Diet Daily Food Plans can be translated into a wide variety of satisfying and unusual meals. To get you started, following are sample menus for each plan to show you how to do just that. After each plan's menus are simple, tasty recipes. Some recipes are used in the menus, and others give you ideas for appetizers, beverages, main courses, vegetable dishes and desserts. For easy inclusion in your Daily Food Plan, at the end of each recipe you are told the food group equivalents, i.e., how many Dairy Delights or Nature's Treats or other Soup Diet Food Group the recipe contains.

Because the amount per serving is too small to count, foods may appear in some recipes without mention of the appropriate food group equivalents. For example, if you use ½ cup of milk in a recipe that makes 8 servings, there's no need for you to worry about counting that small amount of milk in your Daily Food Plan. Small amounts of foods used in this way will not affect your weight loss or weight-control efforts. However, this does *not* mean that you can ignore *nibbles* of small amounts of foods.

The menus and recipes also do not allow the use of salt, except where indicated. Feel free to create your own recipes, but use salt only when called for in the Soup Diet recipes. Use Flexi-Foods or Freebies to flavor your foods.

Eating with others can add extra "flavor" to a meal, too. The Soup Diet provides you with recipes that, in general, make 4 servings each. If you do not share meals, then freeze leftover portions when possible. This will help save food preparation time—and money, too! When recipes call for one-half can of soup, use the other half in your next meal or the next day.

The Kick-Off Diet recipes can be used in all three plans. To simplify using them in the Take-It-Off and Keep-It-Off-Forever Plans, the food group equivalents for each recipe are included at the end of this chapter. Recipes for the Take-It-Off Plan can also be used when you are following the Keep-It-Off-Forever Plan.

TAKE-IT-OFF PLAN 1200 CALORIE FOOD PLAN

Sample Menu Day 1

FOOD GROUPS	BREAKFAST OR MIDMORNING SNACK	FOR 1500 CALORIES CHANGE AMOUNTS AS FOLLOWS
1 Nature's Treat	Fresh grapefruit half with mint sprig	Increase to:
1¼ Nature's Treats	1 oven-warmed Banana Raisin Muffin*	2 oven-warmed Banana Raisin Muffins* spread with 2 teaspoons margarine (Adds 1 Complex Carb, ¼ Protein Provider, 1½ Palate Pleasers, 1¼ Nature's Treats)
1 Complex Carb	spread with	
¼ Protein Provider	1 teaspoon margarine	
1½ Palate Pleasers		
1 Dairy Delight	1 cup frosty cold skim milk	
Freebie	Steaming hot coffee or tea	

LUNCH

1 Soup Group	1 cup prepared Campbell's Chicken Alphabet Soup	
	Garden Cottage Salad (¼ cup	
1 Protein Provider	lowfat cottage cheese and chopped	
Ad Lib Veggies	green pepper, celery and radish,	
1 Protein Provider	seasoned with dill, served on fresh	
1 Palate Pleaser	lettuce bed, garnished with 1 chopped hard-cooked egg, covered with 1 teaspoon oil mixed with 1 teaspoon herbed vinegar)	
1 Complex Carb	3 crisp rye wafers	
1 Nature's Treat	½ cup chilled unsweetened pineapple chunks	Increase to: ¾ cup pineapple chunks (Adds ½ Nature's Treat)
Freebie	Steaming hot coffee or tea	

114

DINNER

3 Protein Providers
2 Complex Carbs
1/2 Palate Pleaser
Ad Lib Veggies
1 Limited Veggie

3 ounces broiled lean hamburger patty on toasted bun with 1 teaspoon mayonnaise, tomato slice and fresh lettuce leaves 1/2 cup diced beets marinated in wine vinegar

Increase to:
4 ounces broiled lean hamburger patty (Adds 1 Protein Provider)

Increase to:
1 cup diced beets (Adds 1 Limited Veggie).

1 Dairy Delight

1/2 cup chilled lowfat plain yogurt, seasoned with ginger

Freebie

Bubbly mineral water over ice with slice of fresh lime

SNACK

1 Soup Group

1 cup prepared Campbell's Vegetable Beef Soup

TOTAL SERVINGS OF FOOD GROUPS FOR DAY 1

1200 Calorie Meal Plan:
2 Dairy Delights
2+ Ad Lib Veggies
1 Limited Veggie
3 1/4 Nature's Treats
4 Complex Carbs
5 1/4 Protein Providers
3 Palate Pleasers
2 Soup Group

1500 Calorie Meal Plan:
2 Dairy Delights
2+ Ad Lib Veggies
2 Limited Veggies
5 Nature's Treats
5 Complex Carbs
6 1/2 Protein Providers
4 1/2 Palate Pleasers
2 Soup Group

TAKE-IT-OFF PLAN 1200 CALORIE FOOD PLAN

Sample Menu Day 2

FOOD GROUPS	BREAKFAST OR MIDMORNING SNACK	FOR 1500 CALORIES CHANGE AMOUNTS AS FOLLOWS
1 Complex Carb 1½ Nature's Treats	½ cup cooked oatmeal topped with 3 tablespoons raisins, cinnamon to taste	Add: 1 slice whole wheat toast (Adds 1 Complex Carb)
1 Dairy Delight Freebie	1 cup frosty cold skim milk Steaming hot coffee or tea	1 teaspoon margarine (Adds 1 Palate Pleaser)

LUNCH

1 Soup Group	1 cup prepared Campbell's Beef Noodle Soup	Add: 1 medium tangerine (Adds
2 Protein Providers ¼ Dairy Delight ½ Nature's Treat	1 serving Polynesian Chicken Salad* on	1 Nature's Treat)
Ad Lib Veggies 1 Complex Carb 1 Palate Pleaser Freebie	crisp lettuce bed ½ small pita bread spread with 1 teaspoon margarine Bubbly mineral water over ice with slice of fresh lime	

DINNER

1 Flexi-Food	1/3 cup "V-8" Cocktail Vegetable Juice over ice with slice of fresh lemon	
3 Protein Providers	3 ounces broiled fillet of sole seasoned with paprika	Increase to: 4 ounces broiled fillet of sole (Adds 1 Protein Provider)
1 Complex Carb	1 small baked potato topped with	
1 Palate Pleaser	1 teaspoon margarine and fresh chives	
1 Limited Veggie	1/2 cup tiny green peas	Increase to: 1 cup green peas (Adds 1 Limited Veggie)
Ad Lib Veggies	Tossed fresh spinach covered with	
1 Palate Pleaser	1 teaspoon oil mixed with 2 teaspoons herbed vinegar	2 teaspoons oil (Adds 1 Palate Pleaser)
1 Nature's Treat	1/2 cup unsweetened sliced peaches topped with	Increase to: 1 cup unsweetened sliced peaches (Adds 1 Treat)
1/2 Dairy Delight	1/4 cup frosty cold evaporated skim milk served with	
1 Complex Carb	2 graham cracker squares	
Freebie	Steaming hot coffee or tea	

SNACK

1 Soup Group	1 cup prepared Campbell's Chicken Vegetable Soup

TOTAL SERVINGS OF FOOD GROUPS FOR DAY 2

1200 Calorie Meal Plan:

1¾ Dairy delights	5 Protein Providers
2 + Ad Lib Veggies	3 Palate Pleasers
1 Limited Veggie	1 Flexi-Food
3 Nature's Treats	2 Soup Group
4 Complex Carbs	

1500 Calorie Meal Plan:

1¾ Dairy Delights	6 Protein Providers
2 + Ad Lib Veggies	4 Palate Pleasers
2 Limited Veggies	1 Flexi-Food
5 Nature's Treats	2 Soup Group
5 Complex Carbs	

TAKE-IT-OFF PLAN 1200 CALORIE FOOD PLAN

Sample Menu Day 3

FOOD GROUPS	BRUNCH	FOR 1500 CALORIES CHANGE AMOUNTS AS FOLLOWS
1 Soup Group	1 cup prepared Campbell's Crispy Tomato Garden Soup	
2 Protein Providers	2 eggs scrambled with mixed herbs (tarragon, parsley, chives, marjoram)	Decrease to: 1 egg scrambled with mixed herbs (Subtracts 1 Protein Provider)
2 Complex Carbs	1 toasted English muffin spread with	
1 Palate Pleaser	1 teaspoon margarine	
1 Dairy Delight	Banana Swirl (combine in blender:	
1 Nature's Treat	1 cup skim milk, 1/2 small frozen banana and 1 teaspoon vanilla extract)	Increase to: 1 small frozen banana (Adds 1 Nature's Treat)
Freebie	Steaming hot coffee or tea	

COMPANY DINNER

1 Protein Provider	1 serving Cheese Dip* with fresh celery sticks	
1/2 Dairy Delight		
Ad Lib Veggies		
2 Protein Providers	1 serving Shrimp Kabobs* served over	Increase to: 2 servings Shrimp Kabobs (Adds 2 Protein Providers, 1 Palate Pleaser)
1 Palate Pleaser		
Ad Lib Veggies		
1 Complex Carb	1/2 cup hot and fluffy brown rice seasoned with basil	

118

Ad Lib Veggies	Lightly steamed julienne carrots
1 Palate Pleaser	Lettuce wedge covered with 1 tablespoon reduced-calorie mayonnaise
2 Nature's Treats	1/2 cup fresh or frozen melon balls topped with
1/2 Dairy Delight	1/4 cup plain lowfat yogurt and 1/2 cup fresh or frozen blueberries
Freebie	Jasmine tea

Increase to:
1 cup melon balls (Adds 1 Nature's treat)

Add:
1/2 cup wheat germ to fruit and yogurt (Adds 1 Complex Carb)

SNACK

| 1 Soup Group | 1 cup prepared Campbell's Minestrone Soup |
| 1 Complex Carb | 20 oyster crackers |

TOTAL SERVINGS OF FOOD GROUPS FOR DAY 3

1200 Calorie Meal Plan:
2 Dairy Delights
2 + Ad Lib Veggies
3 Nature's Treats
4 Complex Carbs
5 Protein Providers
3 Palate Pleasers
2 Soup Group

1500 Calorie Meal Plan:
2 Dairy Delights
2 + Ad Lib Veggies
5 Nature's Treats
5 Complex Carbs
6 Protein Providers
4 Palate Pleasers
2 Soup Group

TAKE-IT-OFF PLAN RECIPES

BEVERAGES

Strawberry Banana Shake

³/₄ cup small strawberries
1 cup skim milk
¹/₂ small ripe banana
¹/₈ teaspoon ground nutmeg

In electric blender, combine all ingredients; cover. Blend on high speed until smooth. Pour into glasses; garnish with whole strawberries if desired. Makes 2 servings (1 cup each).

Each serving equals: ¹/₂ Dairy Delight, 1 Nature's Treat

Spiced Cranberry Punch

4 cups cranberry juice cocktail
1 cinnamon stick
¹/₂ teaspoon whole cloves
1 cup cantaloupe balls
1 small apple, cored and chopped
1 bottle (10 ounces) club soda, chilled
Ice cubes

In medium saucepan, heat cranberry juice, cinnamon stick and cloves to boiling. Reduce heat to low; cover. Simmer 10 minutes. Strain; add fruit. Chill. Just before serving, add club soda and ice cubes. Makes 8 servings (³/₄ cup each).

Each serving equals: 2¹/₂ Nature's Treats

APPETIZERS

Shrimp-Topped Cucumber Rounds

$^1/_4$ cup plain lowfat yogurt
$^1/_4$ teaspoon curry powder
$^1/_8$ teaspoon garlic powder
1 small cucumber, cut in 12 slices
12 cooked small shrimp

In small bowl, mix yogurt, curry powder and garlic. Spoon 1 teaspoon yogurt mixture on each cucumber slice; top each with shrimp. Makes 4 servings (3 appetizers each).

Each serving equals: $^3/_4$ Protein Provider

Mexican Eggplant Pizzas

1 can (10$^3/_4$ ounces) condensed tomato soup
2 tablespoons water
1$^1/_2$ teaspoons chili powder
$^1/_8$ teaspoon garlic powder
1 medium eggplant (1 pound), cut in 16 slices
4 ounces shredded reduced-fat process cheese

In small saucepan, combine soup, water, chili and garlic powder; cook over low heat 10 minutes. Stir often.

Meanwhile, on broiler pan, broil eggplant slices 4 inches from heat 6 minutes or until done, turning once. Top each slice with 1 tablespoon soup mixture; sprinkle with 1 tablespoon cheese. Broil 4 inches from heat 1 minute or until cheese melts. Makes 8 servings.

Each serving equals: 1 Protein Provider, 1 Flexi-Food

Stuffed Celery Ribs

1 cup lowfat cottage cheese
2 tablespoons chopped pimiento
1 tablespoon chopped green onions
Dash cayenne pepper
4 stalks celery, cut in 2¹/₂-inch pieces

In small bowl, combine all ingredients except celery; chill. Stuff celery with mixture. Makes 4 servings.

Each serving equals: 1 Protein Provider

Cheese Dip

1 cup plain lowfat yogurt
¹/₂ cup lowfat cottage cheese
2 ounces shredded reduced-fat process cheese
2 tablespoons chopped green onions
2 tablespoons finely chopped green or red
     pepper
¹/₄ teaspoon garlic powder
¹/₄ teaspoon ground cumin
¹/₈ teaspoon pepper

In bowl, combine all ingredients; chill. Serve with fresh vegetables. Makes 4 servings.

Each serving equals: ¹/₂ Dairy Delight, 1 Protein Provider

Chicken Puffs

¹/₂ cup finely chopped cooked chicken
¹/₃ cup reduced-calorie mayonnaise
1 tablespoon grated onion
1 teaspoon Worcestershire sauce
¹/₄ teaspoon thyme leaves, crushed
1 egg white
24 unsalted melba toast rounds

Appetizer: Cheese Dip with Vegetables, Shrimp Topped Cucumbers & Mexican Eggplant Pizzas

In small bowl, mix chicken, mayonnaise, onion, Worcestershire and thyme. Beat egg white until soft peaks form; gently fold into chicken mixture.

Spoon mixture on toast; arrange on broiler pan. Broil 4 inches from heat 1 minute or until lightly browned. Makes 8 servings (3 puffs each).

Each serving equals: ½ Complex Carb, ¼ Protein Provider, ¾ Palate Pleaser

Herbed Buttered Croutons

4 teaspoons softened margarine
¼ teaspoon Italian seasoning, crushed
Dash garlic powder
Dash pepper
4 slices stale whole wheat bread

In small bowl, mix margarine, Italian seasoning, garlic powder and pepper. Spread on bread; cut into ½-inch cubes. Arrange in single layer on jelly-roll pan; bake at 300°F. for 25 minutes or until brown. Stir often. Makes 4 servings (⅔ cup each).

Each serving equals: 1 Complex Carb, 1 Palate Pleaser

Tuna Stuffed Cherry Tomatoes

16 cherry tomatoes
1 can (3¼ ounces) tuna packed in water
2 tablespoons plain lowfat yogurt
1 teaspoon grated onion
¼ teaspoon grated lemon rind
1 teaspoon chopped fresh parsley

Thinly slice tops from tomatoes; hollow out. In small bowl, combine remaining ingredients; spoon into tomatoes. Chill. Makes 4 servings (4 tomatoes each).

Each serving equals: ¾ Protein Provider

SALADS AND SALAD DRESSINGS

Creamy Four-Herb Salad Dressing

*1 can (10³/4 ounces) condensed tomato garden
        soup
¹/₂ cup plain lowfat yogurt
1 small clove garlic, minced
1 tablespoon chopped fresh parsley
¹/₄ teaspoon ground thyme
¹/₄ teaspoon rosemary leaves, crushed
¹/₄ teaspoon rubbed sage*

In covered jar or shaker, combine ingredients; chill. Shake well
before using. Makes 12 servings (2 tablespoons each).

Each serving equals: ³/4 Flexi-Food

Spiced Yogurt Fruit Dressing

*1 cup plain lowfat yogurt
¹/₄ teaspoon grated orange rind
2 tablespoons orange juice
1 teaspoon vanilla extract
¹/₄ teaspoon ground cinnamon
¹/₈ teaspoon ground nutmeg*

In small bowl, combine all ingredients; chill. Makes 4 servings
(¹/4 cup each).

Each serving equals: ¹/2 Dairy Delight

Fruit Mold

4 teaspoons unflavored gelatin
2¹/₂ cups orange juice
1 can (8 ounces) crushed pineapple in
*   pineapple juice*
¹/₂ cup sliced strawberries
¹/₂ cup seedless green grapes (12 grapes), cut
*   in half*

In saucepan, sprinkle gelatin over orange juice to soften. Place over low heat, stirring until gelatin is dissolved. Chill until slightly thickened; fold in remaining ingredients. Pour into 1-quart mold; chill 1 hour or until firm. Unmold on serving plate. Makes 8 servings (¹/₂ cup each).

Each serving equals: 1 Nature's Treat

Fresh Fruit Medley

1 can (8 ounces) chunk pineapple in pineapple
*   juice*
¹/₂ small banana, sliced
¹/₃ cup seedless green grapes (8 grapes)
¹/₃ cup sliced strawberries
¹/₄ teaspoon ground cinnamon

In bowl, combine all ingredients; chill. Makes 4 servings (¹/₃ cup each).

Each serving equals: 1 Nature's Treat

SIDE DISHES

Ratatouille Stuffed Zucchini

2 small zucchini squash
1 small tomato, chopped (³/₄ cup)
¹/₂ cup chopped peeled eggplant
¹/₂ cup chopped green pepper
2 tablespoons grated onion
1 clove garlic, minced
¹/₂ teaspoon oregano leaves, crushed
¹/₈ teaspoon pepper
3 tablespoons grated Parmesan cheese
¹/₂ cup water

Cut zucchini in half lengthwise; scoop out pulp leaving ¹/₄-inch shell. Coarsely chop pulp.

In covered nonstick skillet or skillet sprayed with nonstick cooking spray, cook tomato, eggplant, green pepper and onion with garlic, oregano, pepper and zucchini pulp until vegetables are tender.

Spoon into zucchini shells. Sprinkle with cheese. Arrange in 1¹/₂-quart shallow baking dish (10x6x2″); pour water in bottom of dish. Cover; bake at 375°F. 30 minutes or until done. Makes 4 servings.

Each serving equals: ¹/₄ Protein Provider

Vegetable Cheese Melt

2 cups fresh or frozen broccoli flowerets
2 cups fresh or frozen cauliflowerets
1 cup sliced carrots
4 teaspoons margarine
4 teaspoons all-purpose flour
²/₃ cup skim milk
4 ounces shredded reduced-fat process cheese

In medium saucepan, in 1 inch boiling water, heat vegetables to boil. Reduce heat to low; cover. Simmer 5 minutes or until tender-crisp; drain.

Meanwhile, in small saucepan, melt margarine; blend in flour. Cook a few minutes, stirring constantly. Remove from heat. Add milk, a little at a time, stirring until smooth after each addition.

Cook, stirring until thickened. Add cheese; heat, stirring until cheese melts. Serve over vegetables. Makes 4 servings (1 cup each).

Each serving equals: ¼ Complex Carb, 1 Protein Provider, 1 Palate Pleaser

Vegetable Medley

½ can (10½-ounce size) condensed French
    onion soup
Water
¼ teaspoon rosemary leaves, crushed
1 cup celery cut in thin sticks (2 inches long)
1 cup sliced zucchini squash
1 cup thinly sliced carrots
1 cup green pepper strips
1 tablespoon cornstarch

In medium saucepan over medium heat, heat soup, ½ cup water and rosemary to boiling. Add vegetables; heat to boiling. Reduce heat to low; cover. Simmer 3 minutes or until tender-crisp. With slotted spoon transfer vegetables to serving dish; keep warm.

In bowl, mix cornstarch and 2 tablespoons water; add to soup mixture. Cook, stirring until thickened. Pour over vegetables. Makes 4 servings (1 cup each).

Each serving equals: 1 Flexi-Food

Vegetable Cheese Melt, Lemon-Herbed Potatoes, Pasta Primavera & Stir-Fried Chicken & Vegetables

Lemon-Herbed New Potatoes

1 pound small new potatoes
2 tablespoons melted margarine
1 tablespoon fresh lemon juice
1/2 teaspoon dried dill weed or 2 teaspoons
   chopped fresh dill
1/4 teaspoon salt
1/8 teaspoon pepper

Peel thin strip around center of potatoes. In medium saucepan, in 1 inch boiling water, heat potatoes to boiling. Reduce heat to low; cover.

   Simmer 15 minutes or until tender. Drain. Toss hot potatoes with remaining ingredients. Makes 4 servings.

Each serving equals: 1 Complex Carb, 1 1/2 Palate Pleasers

MAIN DISHES

South of the Border Chicken

2 whole chicken breasts, split, skinned and
   boned (1 pound boneless)
1/2 can (10 1/2-ounce size) condensed vegetable
   soup
1/2 cup chopped green pepper
1/4 cup chopped onion
1 large clove garlic, minced
1 1/2 teaspoons chili powder
1/8 teaspoon pepper
1/4 cup water
2 teaspoons all-purpose flour

In nonstick skillet or skillet sprayed with nonstick cooking spray, brown chicken. Add soup, wine, green pepper, onion, garlic, chili and pepper.

Cover; cook over low heat 10 minutes or until done. Stir occasionally.

Gradually blend water into flour until smooth; slowly stir into soup mixture. Cook, stirring until thickened. Makes 4 servings.

Each serving equals: 3 Protein Providers, 1 Flexi-Food

Spicy Fruited Chicken

*2 whole chicken breasts, split, skinned and
    boned (1 pound boneless)*
*1/2 can (10³/4-ounce size) condensed chicken
    broth*
1 tablespoon Worcestershire sauce
1/4 teaspoon ground ginger
*1 can (16 ounces) sliced peaches in
    unsweetened juice*
2 tablespoons chopped green onions
2 tablespoons all-purpose flour

In large nonstick skillet or skillet sprayed with nonstick cooking spray, brown chicken. Stir in chicken broth, Worcestershire and ginger.

Cover; cook over low heat 15 minutes until done. Stir occasionally.

Drain peaches, reserving juice; add peaches and onions to chicken.

Gradually blend reserved peach juice into flour until smooth; slowly stir into chicken mixture. Cook, stirring until thickened. Makes 4 servings.

Each serving equals: 1/2 Nature's Treat, 1/4 Complex Carb, 3
                  Protein Providers, 1 Flexi-Food

Polynesian Chicken Salad

1¹/₂ cups chopped cooked chicken (8 ounces)
1 can (8 ounces) crushed pineapple in
*   pineapple juice*
¹/₂ cup plain lowfat yogurt
¹/₄ cup chopped green onions
¹/₄ teaspoon ground ginger
¹/₄ teaspoon salt
¹/₈ teaspoon pepper

In bowl, combine all ingredients; chill. Makes 4 servings (¹/₂ cup each).

Each serving equals: ¹/₄ Dairy Delight, ¹/₂ Nature's Treat, 1¹/₂ Protein Providers

Stir-Fried Chicken and Vegetables

¹/₂ can (10¹/₂-ounce size) condensed French
*   onion soup*
¹/₄ cup water
1 tablespoon cornstarch
¹/₂ teaspoon basil leaves, crushed
¹/₄ teaspoon thyme leaves, crushed
¹/₈ teaspoon pepper
2 whole chicken breasts, skinned and boned
*   (1 pound boneless), cut in ¹/₂-inch pieces*
1 cup green pepper strips
1 cup sliced zucchini squash
1 medium tomato, cut in 8 wedges

To make marinade, in shallow dish, combine soup, water, cornstarch, basil, thyme and pepper; add chicken. Toss well; chill 30 minutes or more.

In large nonstick skillet or skillet sprayed with nonstick cooking spray, cook green pepper and zucchini 5 minutes until tender-crisp. Remove from skillet and set aside.

Add chicken with marinade to skillet; cook 10 minutes until chicken is done and sauce is thickened. Stir often.

Return cooked vegetables and tomato to skillet. Heat; stir occasionally. Makes 4 servings (1½ cups each).

Each serving equals: 3 Protein Providers, 1 Flexi-Food

Pork Chops à l'Orange

4 pork chops, about ³/₄ inch thick (1¹/₄ pounds)
2 teaspoons vegetable oil
1 cup orange juice
1 teaspoon Worcestershire sauce
¹/₈ teaspoon salt
¹/₈ teaspoon pepper
1 cup green pepper strips
1 cup fresh orange sections
1 tablespoon cornstarch
3 tablespoons water

Trim fat from chops. In skillet, brown pork chops in oil. Pour off fat. Add orange juice, Worcestershire, salt and pepper. Cover; cook over low heat 25 minutes, spooning juice mixture over chops occasionally.

Add green pepper and orange sections; cook 5 minutes more or until done. Transfer pork chops to serving platter; keep warm.

In small bowl, combine cornstarch and water; add to juice mixture. Cook, stirring until thickened. Serve with pork chops. Makes 4 servings.

Each serving equals: 1 Nature's Treat, 3 Protein Providers, ½ Palate Pleaser

Pork Ragoût

*1 pound boneless pork shoulder, cut in ³/₄-inch
    cubes*
4 teaspoons vegetable oil
*¹/₂ can (10³/₄-ounce size) condensed tomato
    soup*
³/₄ cup water
¹/₂ cup sliced celery
¹/₂ cup chopped onion
1 large clove garlic, minced
¹/₂ teaspoon caraway seed
¹/₄ teaspoon pepper

Trim fat from pork. In saucepan, brown pork in oil. Pour off fat.
Add remaining ingredients; heat to boiling. Reduce heat to low;
cover.

Simmer 1 hour or until done; stir occasionally. Makes 4
servings (¹/₂ cup each).

Each serving equals: 3 Protein Providers, 1 Palate Pleaser, 1
Flexi-Food

Vegetable Stuffed Meat Loaf

1 pound lean ground beef
1¹/₄ cups fresh bread crumbs
¹/₄ cup skim milk
2 eggs, slightly beaten
1 teaspoon oregano leaves, crushed
1 teaspoon Worcestershire sauce
¹/₈ teaspoon pepper
¹/₈ teaspoon hot pepper sauce
1 cup chopped cooked carrots

In bowl, mix ground beef, 1 cup bread crumbs, milk, 1 egg,
oregano, Worcestershire, pepper and hot pepper sauce. In
another bowl, combine carrots, remaining ¹/₄ cup bread crumbs
and remaining egg.

On broiler pan, shape half meat mixture firmly into 5-inch
round. Make well in center; fill with carrot mixture. Top with
remaining meat mixture. Press firmly together; seal edges.

Bake at 350°F. for 45 minutes or until done. Serve with additional hot pepper sauce. Makes 4 servings.

Each serving equals: 3½ Protein Providers, 2 Complex Carbs

Stuffed Green Peppers

*½ can (10¾-ounce size) condensed tomato
    soup
2 tablespoons water
1½ teaspoons marjoram leaves, crushed
1 teaspoon garlic powder
4 large green peppers
1 pound lean ground beef
¼ cup chopped onion
⅛ teaspoon pepper
1 cup cooked rice (prepared without salt)
2 ounces shredded reduced-fat process cheese*

To make sauce, in small saucepan, combine soup, water, ½ teaspoon marjoram and ½ teaspoon garlic powder; cook over low heat 10 minutes. Stir often.

Meanwhile, remove tops and seeds from peppers. In large saucepan, in 1 inch boiling water, heat peppers to boiling.

Reduce heat to low; cover. Simmer 10 minutes or until tender-crisp; drain. Arrange in 1½-quart shallow baking dish (10 × 6 × 2″).

To make filling, in nonstick skillet or skillet sprayed with nonstick cooking spray, brown ground beef and cook onion with pepper, remaining 1 teaspoon marjoram and remaining ½ teaspoon garlic powder until tender; stir to separate meat.

Pour off fat. Add rice and 2 tablespoons sauce. Spoon filling into peppers; top with remaining sauce. Sprinkle with cheese.

Cover; bake at 375°F. for 30 minutes or until done. Makes 4 servings.

Each serving equals: ½ Complex Carb, 3½ Protein Providers,
1 Flexi-Food

Shrimp Kabobs

4 teaspoons vegetable oil
¹/₄ teaspoon grated lemon rind
1 tablespoon fresh lemon juice
1 tablespoon water
¹/₄ teaspoon garlic powder
Dash crushed red pepper
1 pound medium shrimp (24), shelled and
*   deveined*
1 large green pepper, cut in 16 squares
12 small whole fresh mushrooms

To make marinade, in shallow dish, combine oil, lemon rind, lemon juice, water, garlic powder and red pepper; add shrimp. Toss well; chill 30 minutes or more.

Meanwhile, in small saucepan, in 1 inch boiling water, cook green pepper 1 minute; drain. Remove shrimp from marinade, reserving marinade.

On each of 4 skewers, arrange shrimp, green pepper and mushrooms. Place on broiler pan. Broil 4 inches from heat 10 minutes or until done, turning often and brushing with marinade. Makes 4 servings.

Each serving equals: 2 Protein Providers, 1 Palate Pleaser

Lemon Tarragon Broiled Fillets

4 teaspoons melted margarine
1 tablespoon fresh lemon juice
¹/₂ teaspoon tarragon leaves, crushed
¹/₈ teaspoon pepper
1 pound fillets of flounder or sole

Line broiler pan with foil; spray with nonstick cooking spray. In small bowl, combine margarine, lemon juice, tarragon and pepper.

Arrange fillets in single layer on broiler pan; broil 4 inches from heat 5 minutes or until done, brushing often with lemon mixture. Makes 4 servings.

Each serving equals: 3 Protein Providers, 1 Palate Pleaser

Tuna Soufflé

2 tablespoons chopped green onions
2 tablespoons finely chopped red or green
    pepper
8 teaspoons margarine
1/4 cup all-purpose flour
1 cup skim milk
4 eggs, separated
1 can (6 1/2 ounces) tuna packed in water,
    drained
2 teaspoons fresh lemon juice
1/2 teaspoon dried dill weed or 2 teaspoons
    chopped fresh dill
1/4 teaspoon salt
1/8 teaspoon pepper
1/4 teaspoon cream of tartar

In saucepan, cook onions and red or green pepper in margarine until tender; blend in flour. Cook a few minutes, stirring constantly. Remove from heat. Add milk, a little at a time, stirring until smooth after each addition. Cook, stirring until thickened.

Beat egg yolks until thick and lemon-colored; gradually stir in about 2 tablespoons milk mixture. Stir into saucepan. Cook 1 minute, stirring (do not boil).

Add tuna, lemon, dill, salt and pepper. Cover tightly; cool.

In large bowl, using clean beater, beat egg whites until foamy; add cream of tartar. Beat until stiff peaks form; fold in tuna mixture.

Pour into 1 1/2-quart casserole or soufflé dish. Bake at 350° F. for 45 minutes or until light brown. Serve immediately. Makes 4 servings.

Each serving equals: 1/4 Dairy Delight, 1/2 Complex Carb, 2 Protein Providers, 2 Palate Pleasers

Pasta Primavera

4 ounces uncooked linguine
1 cup fresh or frozen cut green beans
¹/₂ cup coarsely chopped green pepper
¹/₂ cup coarsely chopped red pepper
1 medium clove garlic, minced
4 teaspoons margarine
¹/₂ can (10¹/₂-ounce size) condensed French
*   onion soup*
2 teaspoons cornstarch

Cook linguine in unsalted water following package directions; drain.

Meanwhile, in small saucepan, in 1 inch boiling water, heat green beans to boiling. Reduce heat to low; cover. Simmer 5 minutes or until tender-crisp; drain.

In skillet cook green and red pepper with garlic in margarine until tender-crisp. Add soup and cornstarch. Cook, stirring until thickened. Serve over linguine. Makes 4 servings.

Each serving equals: 1 Complex Carb, 1 Palate Pleaser, 1 Flexi-Food

Zucchini Lasagne

9 lasagne noodles
1 can (10³/₄ ounces) condensed tomato soup
¹/₃ cup water
1 clove garlic, minced
1¹/₂ teaspoons basil leaves, crushed
4 cups sliced zucchini squash
2 cups sliced fresh mushrooms
¹/₂ cup chopped onion
1 cup lowfat cottage cheese (8 ounces)
6 tablespoons grated Parmesan cheese

Cook noodles in unsalted water following package directions.

Meanwhile, to make sauce, in small saucepan, combine soup, water, garlic and 1 teaspoon basil; heat to boiling. Reduce heat to low; cover. Simmer 10 minutes; stir occasionally.

In nonstick skillet or skillet sprayed with nonstick cooking spray, cook zucchini, mushrooms, onion and remaining ½ teaspoon basil 7 minutes or until tender-crisp.

In 2-quart shallow baking dish (12 × 8 × 2″), spoon 4 table-spoons sauce. Arrange 3 alternate layers of noodles, cottage cheese, vegetable mixture, sauce and Parmesan cheese.

Cover; bake at 350°F. for 30 minutes or until hot. Makes 8 servings.

Each serving equals: 1 Complex Carb, ¾ Protein Provider, 1
Flexi-Food

Spinach Cheese Strata

8 slices whole wheat bread
4 ounces shredded reduced-fat process cheese
1 package (10 ounces) frozen chopped
spinach, cooked and well drained
4 eggs, slightly beaten
1¼ cups skim milk
⅛ teaspoon pepper

Cut each slice bread into 4 triangles. In 2-quart shallow baking dish (12x8x2″) sprayed with nonstick cooking spray, arrange half the bread triangles, covering bottom of dish. Sprinkle with half the cheese; top with spinach. Cover with remaining bread triangles.

In bowl, combine eggs, milk and pepper; pour over bread; sprinkle with remaining cheese. Cover; chill 1 hour or more.

Uncover; bake at 325°F. for 35 minutes or until set. Makes 4 servings.

Each serving equals: ¼ Dairy Delight, 2 Complex Carbs, 2
Protein Providers

Savory Lentils

½ can (10½-ounce size) condensed beef broth
1½ cups water
1 cup dried lentils, washed and sorted
¼ cup chopped celery
¼ cup chopped onion
¼ cup chopped red or green pepper
1 large clove garlic, minced
½ teaspoon thyme leaves, crushed
⅛ teaspoon pepper
1 small bay leaf

In saucepan, combine all ingredients. Cover; bring to boil. Reduce heat to low; simmer 30 minutes or until done. Stir occasionally. Remove bay leaf. Makes 4 servings (¾ cup each).

Each serving equals: 1 Complex Carb or 2 Protein Providers, 1 Flexi-Food

DESERTS

Glazed Cheese Pie

Cereal Pie Crust (recipe below)
1 can (8 ounces) chunk pineapple in pineapple
*   juice*
1 envelope unflavored gelatin
1/4 cup water
1 1/2 cups lowfat cottage cheese
1/2 teaspoon grated orange rind
1/8 teaspoon ground nutmeg
2 teaspoons cornstarch
2/3 cup unsweetened pineapple juice
3 kiwi fruit, peeled and thinly sliced

Prepare pie crust. Drain pineapple, reserving juice.

In small saucepan, sprinkle gelatin over water and reserved pineapple juice to soften. Place over low heat, stirring until gelatin is dissolved.

Pour into electric blender; add pineapple chunks, cottage cheese, orange rind and nutmeg. Cover; blend on high speed until smooth. Pour into bowl. Refrigerate until mixture mounds when dropped from spoon.

Spread mixture in prepared pie crust; chill until set.

Meanwhile, in small saucepan, mix cornstarch with 2/3 cup pineapple juice. Cook, stirring until thickened. Arrange kiwi on pie; spoon cornstarch mixture evenly over kiwi. Chill. Makes 8 servings.

Cereal Pie Crust

1 cup oven-toasted rice cereal
1/2 cup wheat germ
8 teaspoons melted margarine

On waxed paper with rolling pin, crush cereal to make fine crumbs. In bowl, combine crushed cereal, wheat germ and margarine. Spoon into 9" pie plate; using back of spoon, press firmly into pie plate. Bake at 350°F. for 8 minutes or until browned; cool. Makes one 9" pie crust.

Each serving equals: 1 Nature's Treat, ½ Complex Carb, ¾ Protein Provider, 1 Palate Pleaser

Oatmeal Date Cookies

2 tablespoons softened margarine
1 egg, slightly beaten
1 tablespoon water
½ teaspoon vanilla extract
¼ cup all-purpose flour
½ teaspoon baking powder
½ teaspoon ground cinnamon
8 pitted dates, finely chopped
⅓ cup quick-cooking oats, uncooked

Preheat oven to 350°F. In medium bowl, beat margarine, egg, water and vanilla; stir in flour, baking powder, cinnamon, dates and oats. Mix well. Drop rounded teaspoonfuls 1 inch apart on nonstick cookie sheet or cookie sheet sprayed with nonstick cooking spray.

Bake 10 minutes or until lightly browned. Cool on rack. Makes 4 servings (3 cookies per serving).

Each serving equals: 1 Nature's Treat, ¾ Complex Carb, 1 Protein Provider, 1½ Palate Pleasers

Broiled Orange Halves

¼ teaspoon ground cinnamon
2 small oranges, cut in half
2 teaspoons melted margarine

Sprinkle cinnamon on orange halves; drizzle each with ½ teaspoon margarine. Arrange on broiler pan; broil 4 inches from heat 3 minutes until lightly browned. Makes 4 servings.

Each serving equals: ½ Nature's Treat, ½ Palate Pleaser

Dessert: Glazed Cheese Pie, Broiled Sunshine Halves, Oatmeal Date Cookies

Banana Raisin Muffins

1 egg, beaten
1 1/2 small bananas, mashed
1/4 cup skim milk
2 teaspoons vegetable oil
2/3 cup all-purpose flour
1 teaspoon baking powder
1/2 teaspoon ground cinnamon
1/8 teaspoon ground cloves
1/4 cup raisins

In small bowl, mix egg, bananas, milk and oil.

In medium bowl, combine flour, baking powder, cinnamon and cloves; add banana mixture. Stir until flour is just moistened; fold in raisins. In 4 nonstick muffin cups or cups sprayed with nonstick cooking spray, spoon batter.

Bake at 425°F. for 20 minutes or until brown and toothpick inserted in center comes out clean. Makes 4 servings.

Each serving equals: 1 1/4 Nature's Treats, 1 1/4 Complex Carbs, 1/4 Protein Provider, 1/2 Palate Pleaser

Creamy Cantaloupe Sherbet

2 cups chopped cantaloupe
1/2 teaspoon fresh lemon or lime juice
1/4 cup skim milk
Dash ground nutmeg

In electric blender, combine all ingredients; cover. Blend on high speed until smooth. Pour into bowl. Cover; freeze until firm. Stir occasionally.

On medium speed of electric mixer, beat until smooth but still frozen. Freeze until firm. Let stand at room temperature 10 minutes before serving. Makes 4 servings (1/2 cup each).

Each serving equals: 1 Nature's Treat

Gingered Pineapple Crepes

3 tablespoons all-purpose flour
1 egg, slightly beaten
1/2 cup skim milk
1 1/2 teaspoons vegetable oil
1 can (8 ounces) crushed pineapple in
*   pineapple juice*
2 tablespoons raisins
2 teaspoons cornstarch
1/4 teaspoon ground ginger

To make batter, in bowl, beat flour and egg; gradually beat in milk and oil until well blended. Chill 1 hour.

To make filling, in small saucepan, combine pineapple with its juice, raisins, cornstarch and ginger. Cook, stirring until thickened.

To make crepes, over low heat, heat 6″ nonstick skillet or skillet or crepe pan sprayed with nonstick cooking spray. Pour 1/4 cup batter into skillet, tipping skillet quickly to coat bottom. Cook over low heat 3 minutes or until top is set and underside is lightly browned. Turn crepe; cook 1 minute more or until underside is golden.

Spoon 1/4 cup filling on each crepe; roll up. Keep warm. Makes 2 servings (2 crepes per serving).

Each serving equals: 1/4 Dairy Delight, 1 1/2 Nature's Treats,
1 Complex Carb, 1/2 Protein Provider,
3/4 Palate Pleaser

Spiced Poached Pears

1 1/3 cups unsweetened pineapple juice
1 cinnamon stick (1 inch)
1/2 teaspoon whole cloves
4 small pears with stems, peeled

In saucepan, heat pineapple juice, cinnamon stick and cloves to boiling. Reduce heat to low; cover. Simmer 10 minutes.

Meanwhile, core pears from bottom end, leaving stem end intact. Add pears to pineapple mixture; cover. Simmer 20 minutes or until just tender. Remove cinnamon stick and cloves. Makes 4 servings.

Each serving equals: 2 Nature's Treats

KEEP-IT-OFF-FOREVER PLAN 1700 CALORIE FOOD PLAN

Sample Menu Day 1

FOOD GROUP	BREAKFAST OR MIDMORNING SNACK	FOR 2000 CALORIES CHANGE AMOUNTS AS FOLLOWS	FOR 2200 CALORIES CHANGE AMOUNTS AS FOLLOWS
1 Complex Carb 1 Nature's Treat 1 Dairy Delight	¾ cup crunchy cornflakes topped with 2 tablespoons chewy raisins covered with 1 cup frosty cold skim milk		
1 Complex Carb 1 Palate Pleaser Freebie	1 slice crisp rye toast spread with 1 teaspoon margarine Steaming hot coffee or tea		
	LUNCH		
1 Nature's Treat 1 Dairy Delight 1 Protein Provider	Apricot Yogurt Fizz (combine in blender 4 juicy apricot halves, ½ cup plain lowfat yogurt, 1 egg and ½ cup club soda)	Increase to: 8 apricot halves (Adds 1 Nature's Treat) Add: ¼ cup wheat germ to salad (Adds 1 Complex Carb)	Add: ⅓ cup nonfat dry milk powder to Apricot Fizz (Adds 1 Dairy Delight)
Ad Lib Veggies 2 Protein Providers 1 Palate Pleaser 1 Complex Carb	Greek Salad (crisp salad greens topped with ½ cup farmer's cheese, cucumber slices, tomato wedges, 2 teaspoons herbed vinegar and 1 teaspoon olive oil) 4 crispy flatbread wafers	Increase to: 2 teaspoons olive oil (Adds 1 Palate Pleaser)	

146

DINNER

1 Soup Group	1 cup prepared Campbell's Chili Beef Soup with	
1 Complex Carb 1 Palate Pleaser	1 2-inch cube of cornbread	Add: 1 teaspoon margarine (Adds 1 Palate Pleaser)
3 Protein Providers Ad Lib Veggies 1 Palate Pleaser 1 Flexi-Food	1 serving Rio Grande Eggplant Casserole*	
1 Complex Carb 1 Palate Pleaser	1 serving Hot and Spicy Rice*	
Ad Lib Veggies 1 Palate Pleaser	Mixed crisp green salad with Lemon Garlic Dressing (Mix 1 teaspoon oil, 1 tablespoon lemon juice and 1 minced garlic clove)	Increase to: 2 teaspoons oil (Adds 1 Palate Pleaser)
1 Nature's Treat	1/2 cup refreshing orange sections drizzled with rum extract	Increase to: 1 cup orange sections (Adds 1 Nature's Treat)
Freebie	Espresso	

SNACK

1 Nature's Treat	1/3 cup chilled apple juice over ice	Increase to: 2/3 cup apple juice (Adds 1 Nature's Treat) Increase to: 1 cup apple juice (Adds 1 Nature's Treat)
2 Fling Foods—Complex Carbs	1 plain cupcake without icing topped with 1/4 cup pineapple sherbet	Increase to: 1/2 cup pineapple sherbet (Adds 1 Fling Food—Complex Carb)

TOTAL SERVINGS OF FOOD GROUPS FOR DAY 1

1700 calorie Meal Plan		2000 calorie Meal Plan		2200 calorie Meal Plan	
2 Dairy Delights	6 Protein Providers	2 Dairy Delights	6 Protein Providers	3 Dairy Delights	6 Protein Providers
2 + Ad Lib Veggies	6 Palate Pleasers	2 + Ad Lib Veggies	7 Palate Pleasers	2 + Ad Lib Veggies	9 Palate Pleasers
4 Nature's Treats	1 Flexi-Food	6 Nature's Treats	1 Flexi-Food	8 Nature's Treats	1 Flexi-Food
7 Complex Carbs	1 Soup Group	8 Complex Carbs	1 Soup Group	9 Complex Carbs	1 Soup Group

KEEP-IT-OFF-FOREVER PLAN 1700 CALORIE FOOD PLAN

Sample Menu Day 2

FOOD GROUP	BREAKFAST OR MIDMORNING SNACK	FOR 2000 CALORIES CHANGE AMOUNTS AS FOLLOWS	FOR 2200 CALORIES CHANGE AMOUNTS AS FOLLOWS
2 Nature's Treats	1 cup chilled orange juice		
1/2 Nature's Treat	1 serving Peanut Apple Treats*		
2 Complex Carbs			
1 Protein Provider			
2 Palate Pleasers			
1 Dairy Delight	1 cup frosty cold skim milk		
Freebie	Steaming hot coffee or tea		
	LUNCH		
1 Soup Group	1 cup prepared Campbell's Cream of Asparagus Soup, made with 1/2 cup skim milk, topped with 1/4 cup plain lowfat yogurt		
1 Dairy Delight			
2 Protein Providers	2 ounces roasted chicken breast, sliced on 2 slices pumpernickel bread topped with sliced fresh tomato and crisp lettuce leaves		
2 Complex Carbs			
Ad Lib Veggies		Add:	Add:
Ad Lib Veggies	1 cup shredded fresh cabbage mixed with 1/4 cup unsweetened crushed pineapple and vinegar and celery seed to taste	2 teaspoons mayonnaise (Adds 1 Palate Pleaser)	2 tablespoons chewy raisins to cabbage-pineapple salad (Adds 1 Nature's Treat)
1/2 Nature's Treat			
Freebie	Bubbly mineral water over ice with 1 teaspoon lemon juice		

DINNER

1 Flexi-Food	1/3 cup chilled Campbell's Tomato Juice over ice with slice of fresh lemon
3 Protein Providers	3 ounces lean roast beef with 1 tablespoon horseradish
2 Complex Carbs 1 Palate Pleaser	1 cup noodles seasoned with 1 teaspoon oil and sprinkled with chopped fresh parsley and chives to taste
Ad Lib Veggies Ad Lib Veggies 1 Palate Pleaser	Lightly steamed broccoli spears Mixed green salad covered with 1 teaspoon salad oil mixed with 2 teaspoons wine vinegar
1 Nature's Treat	1 chilled small orange, cut into wedges
Freebie	Steaming hot coffee or tea

Add:
1 small warmed dinner roll (Adds 1 Complex Carb)

Increase to:
2 teaspoons oil (Adds 1 Palate Pleaser)

Add:
1/4 cup wheat germ and 1 teaspoon oil to broccoli (Adds 1 Complex Carb and 1 Palate Pleaser)

SNACK

1 Complex Carb 2 Palate Pleasers	1 serving Herbed Popcorn*
Freebie	Chilled club soda over ice with slice of fresh lime

Add:
Pineapple Fizz (pour 2/3 cup pineapple juice into large glass, add ice and fill with club soda) (Adds 2 Nature's Treats)

Increase to:
1 cup pineapple juice in Pineapple Fizz and mix in 1/2 cup plain lowfat yogurt (Adds 1 Nature's Treat and 1 Dairy Delight)

TOTAL SERVINGS OF FOOD GROUPS FOR DAY 2

1700 calorie Meal Plan		2000 calorie Meal Plan		2200 calorie Meal Plan	
2 Dairy Delights	6 Protein Providers	2 Dairy Delights	6 Protein Providers	3 Dairy Delights	6 Protein Providers
2 + Ad Lib Veggies	6 Palate Pleasers	2 + Ad Lib Veggies	7 Palate Pleasers	2 + Ad Lib Veggies	9 Palate Pleasers
4 Nature's Treats	1 Flexi-Food	6 Nature's Treats	1 Flexi-Food	8 Nature's Treats	1 Flexi-Food
7 Complex Carbs	1 Soup Group	8 Complex Carbs	1 Soup Group	9 Complex Carbs	1 Soup Group

KEEP-IT-OFF-FOREVER PLAN 1700 CALORIE FOOD PLAN

Sample Menu Day 3

FOOD GROUP	BRUNCH	FOR 2000 CALORIES CHANGE AMOUNTS AS FOLLOWS	FOR 2200 CALORIES CHANGE AMOUNTS AS FOLLOWS
2¼ Nature's Treats	1 serving Spiced Cranberry Punch*	Increase to: 2 servings Spiced Cranberry Punch* (Adds 2¼ Nature's Treats)	Increase to: 2 tablespoons raisins (Adds ½ Nature's Treat)
2 Protein Providers 1 Nature's Treat Ad Lib Veggies ½ Dairy Delight 1 Palate Pleaser Ad Lib Veggies 1 Complex Carb	Chicken Salad Delight (Toss together ½ cup cooked diced chicken, ½ small diced apple, 1 tablespoon chewy raisins, 2 tablespoons chopped celery, 2 tablespoons chopped green pepper, 1 tablespoon thinly sliced green onion		
1 Dairy Delight	and ¼ cup plain lowfat yogurt. Top with 3 tablespoons toasted sliced almonds. Serve on lettuce bed.) 4 crisp thin flatbread wafers Café au Lait*		

150

COMPANY DINNER

4 Protein Providers
1 Complex Carb
1 Palate Pleaser
2 Complex Carbs
2 Palate Pleasers

1 serving Fisherman's Stuffed Flounder*

1 large fresh or frozen ear of corn with 2 teaspoons margarine

Add:
1 small warmed dinner roll
(Adds 1 Complex Carb)

Add:
3 tablespoons toasted sliced almonds
(Adds 1 Palate Pleaser)

Add:
1 cup frosty cold skim milk
(Adds 1 Dairy Delight)

Ad Lib Veggies

Lightly steamed Brussels sprouts sprinkled with lemon juice

Ad Lib Veggies
1/3 Flexi-Food

Crisp tossed sliced cucumber and red radish salad covered with 1 serving Oriental Salad Dressing*

2 Fling Foods—Complex Carbs
2 Fling Foods)
Palate Pleasers
1 Nature's Treat Freebies

1 cup coffee ice cream topped with 1/2 small banana, sliced

Increase to:
1 small banana, sliced
(Adds 1 Nature's Treat)

Lemony iced tea

SNACK

1 Soup Group
1/2 Dairy Delight

1 cup prepared Campbell's Cream of Potato Soup, made with 1/2 cup skim milk, topped with fresh chives

1 Complex Carb

3 crisp rye wafers

Increase to:
6 crisp rye wafers
Add:
2 teaspoons margarine
(Adds 2 Palate Pleasers)

TOTAL SERVINGS OF FOOD GROUPS FOR DAY 3

1700 calorie Meal Plan		2000 calorie Meal Plan		2200 calorie Meal Plan	
2 Dairy Delights	6 Protein Providers	2 Dairy Delights	6 Protein Providers	3 Dairy Delights	6 Protein Providers
2+ Ad Lib Veggies	6 Palate Pleasers	2+ Ad Lib Veggies	7 Palate Pleasers	2+ Ad Lib Veggies	9 Palate Pleasers
4¼ Nature's Treats	1/3 Flexi-Food	6½ Nature's Treats	1/3 Flexi-Food	8 Nature's Treats	1/3 Flexi-Food
7 Complex Carbs	1 Soup Group	8 Complex Carbs	1 Soup Group	9 Complex Carbs	1 Soup Group

Keep-It-Off-Forever Plan Recipes

BREAKFAST FOODS

Peanut Apple Treats

2 English muffins, split and toasted
4 tablespoons peanut butter
1 medium apple, cored and cut in 12 slices
1/4 teaspoon ground cinnamon

Spread each muffin half with 1 tablespoon peanut butter; top with 3 apple slices. Sprinkle with cinnamon. Makes 2 servings (2 halves each).

Each serving equals: 1/2 Nature's Treat, 2 Complex Carbs, 1 Protein Provider, 1 Palate Pleaser

Waffles with Spiced Applesauce

1 egg, slightly beaten
1/2 cup skim milk
2 tablespoons water
4 teaspoons vegetable oil
1 teaspoon vanilla extract
3/4 cup all-purpose flour
1 1/2 teaspoons baking powder
2 cups unsweetened applesauce
1/2 teaspoon ground cinnamon
1/8 teaspoon ground nutmeg
1/4 cup plain lowfat yogurt

Preheat a nonstick waffle iron or iron sprayed with nonstick cooking spray.

To make batter, in bowl, combine egg, milk, water, oil and vanilla; add flour and baking powder. Stir until smooth. Bake as directed by manufacturer.

Meanwhile, in small bowl, combine applesauce, cinnamon and nutmeg. Serve with waffles; top with yogurt. Makes 4 servings.

Each serving equals: ¼ Dairy Delight, 1 Nature's Treat, 1½ Complex Carbs, ¼ Protein Provider, 1 Palate Pleaser

BEVERAGES

Mocha Cream Whip

½ cup skim milk
½ cup coffee ice cream
⅛ teaspoon ground cinnamon

In electric blender, combine all ingredients; cover. Blend on high speed until smooth. Pour into serving glass; serve immediately. Makes 1 serving (1 cup).

Each serving equals: ½ Dairy Delight, 1 Complex Carb, 1 Palate Pleaser

Beefy Bloody Mary Punch

4 cups "V-8" vegetable juice
½ cup clam juice
3 tablespoons fresh lemon juice
2 teaspoons pepper
½ teaspoon hot pepper sauce
Lemon slices

In pitcher, combine all ingredients except lemon slices; chill. Garnish with lemon slices. Makes 10 servings (½ cup each).

Each serving equals: 1 Flexi-Food

Spiced Mocha au Lait

2 teaspoons cocoa
2 teaspoons sugar
1 cup coffee
1 cup hot skim milk

In small saucepan, combine cocoa and sugar; stir in coffee. Place over low heat; cover. Simmer 5 minutes.

Pour half the coffee mixture and half the milk into each of 2 coffee mugs; stir. Serve with cinnamon stick stirrers if desired. Makes 2 servings (1 cup each).

Each serving equals: 1 Dairy Delight, ½ Flexi-Food

Sparkling Pineapple Soda

½ cup orange sherbet
⅔ cup unsweetened pineapple juice, chilled
⅓ cup club soda, chilled

In 12-ounce glass, place sherbet. Pour pineapple juice and club soda over sherbet; serve immediately. Makes 1 serving (1½ cups).

Each serving equals: 2 Nature's Treats, 2 Complex Carbs

Orange Blender Breakfast Drink

¼ cup skim milk
¾ cup orange juice
1 egg
½ teaspoon vanilla extract

In electric blender, combine all ingredients; cover. Blend on high speed until smooth. Serve immediately. Makes 1 serving (1½ cups).

Each serving equals: ¼ Dairy Delight, 1½ Nature's Treats, 1
Protein Provider

*Snack Foods: Herbed Popcorn, Spiced Mocha au Lait, Turkey
Noodle Soup*

Minted Citrus Cooler

*1/2 teaspoon dried mint leaves or 1 1/2
    teaspoons fresh mint leaves
1 1/2 cups orange juice
2 tablespoons fresh lemon juice
1 bottle (10 ounces) club soda, chilled
Ice cubes
4 orange slices*

Tie mint leaves in cheesecloth. In medium saucepan over medium heat, heat orange juice, lemon juice and mint bag to boiling. Reduce heat to low. Cover; simmer 5 minutes. Remove and discard mint bag; chill.

Just before serving, add club soda and ice; garnish with orange. Makes 4 servings (3/4 cup each).

Each serving equals: 3/4 Nature's Treat

APPETIZERS

Alpine Cheese Fondue

*1/2 teaspoon dry mustard
Water
6 tablespoons Chablis or other dry white wine
1 large clove garlic, minced
4 ounces shredded reduced-fat process Swiss
    cheese
1 tablespoon flour
1/2 can (11-ounce size) condensed Cheddar
    cheese soup
3 cups assorted raw vegetables (broccoli,
    cauliflower, carrots, etc.)*

In small bowl, combine mustard and ¼ teaspoon v. 'er; set aside 10 minutes.

Meanwhile, to make fondue, in small saucepan or fondue pot over low heat, heat wine, ¼ cup water and garlic until hot; do not boil.

In small bowl, toss cheese with flour; add to wine mixture, stirring until cheese melts. Add soup and reserved mustard mixture. Heat; stir occasionally.

To serve, spear vegetables with toothpick or fondue fork; dip into fondue. Makes 4 servings (¾ cup vegetables and ⅓ cup sauce each).

Each serving equals: ½ Complex Carb, 1 Protein Provider, 1 Flexi-Food

Herbed Popcorn

8 teaspoons melted margarine
½ teaspoon Italian seasoning, crushed
½ teaspoon garlic powder
2 quarts air-popped popcorn

In small bowl, combine margarine, Italian seasoning and garlic powder; pour over popcorn. Toss well. Makes 4 servings (2 cups each).

Each serving equals: 1 Complex Carb, 2 Palate Pleasers

SALADS AND SALAD DRESSINGS

Oriental Salad Dressing

1 can (10³/₄ ounces) condensed chicken broth
¹/₄ cup red wine vinegar
2 tablespoons sesame seed
¹/₂ teaspoon ground ginger
1 medium clove garlic, minced

Discard fat from chicken broth. In a covered jar or shaker, combine all ingredients; chill. Shake well before using. Makes 12 servings (2 tablespoons each).

Each serving equals: ³/₄ Flexi-Food

Mexicali Salad Dressing

1¹/₃ cups "V-8" vegetable juice
¹/₄ cup distilled vinegar
1¹/₄ teaspoons chili powder
Dash cayenne pepper

In covered jar or shaker, combine all ingredients; chill. Shake well before using. Makes 12 servings (2 tablespoons each).

Each serving equals: ¹/₄ Flexi-Food

Salad: Hearty Macaroni Salad, Chickpea Salad, Tossed Salad, Oriental Salad Dressing & Mexicali Salad Dressing

Creamy Dilled Cucumbers

2 cups thinly sliced peeled cucumbers
1/2 cup finely chopped onion
1/2 cup plain lowfat yogurt
1/4 teaspoon dill weed or 1 teaspoon chopped
     fresh dill
1/8 teaspoon salt
1/8 teaspoon pepper

In bowl, combine all ingredients; toss to coat evenly. Chill. Stir well before serving. Makes 4 servings (1/3 cup each).

Each serving equals: 1/4 Dairy Delight, 1/4 Limited Veggie

Sour Red Cabbage

1/3 cup water
1 1/2 tablespoons vinegar
1 teaspoon caraway seed
1/8 teaspoon salt
1/8 teaspoon pepper
3 cups red cabbage cut in long thin shreds

In medium saucepan, heat water, vinegar, caraway seed, salt and pepper to boiling. Add cabbage; heat to boiling. Reduce heat to low; cover. Simmer 5 minutes or until cabbage is tender-crisp. Makes 4 servings (2/3 cup each).

Each serving equals: Freebies

Macaroni Salad

4 ounces shell macaroni
1/4 cup reduced-calorie mayonnaise
1/4 cup chopped pimiento
1/4 cup finely chopped green pepper
1 teaspoon fresh lemon juice
1/8 teaspoon pepper

Cook macaroni in unsalted water following package directions; cool. In large bowl, toss macaroni with remaining ingredients; chill. Makes 4 servings (3/4 cup each).

Each serving equals: 1 Complex Carb, 1 Palate Pleaser

Chick Pea Salad

8 teaspoons vegetable oil
2¹/₂ teaspoons vinegar
¹/₂ teaspoon oregano leaves, crushed
¹/₈ teaspoon crushed red pepper
2 cups canned chick peas (garbanzo beans)
¹/₂ cup chopped fresh tomato
2 tablespoons chopped onion

In bowl, combine oil, vinegar, oregano and red pepper; toss with chick peas, tomato and onion. Chill. Makes 4 servings (³/₄ cup each).

Each serving equals: 1 Complex Carb or 2 Protein Providers, 2 Palate Pleasers

Layered Cran-Strawberry Nut Mold

2 envelopes unflavored gelatin
3 cups cranberry juice cocktail
1¹/₂ cups sliced fresh strawberries
3 tablespoons chopped walnuts (12 halves)
¹/₂ cup plain lowfat yogurt
Dash ground nutmeg

In saucepan, sprinkle gelatin over cranberry juice to soften. Place over low heat, stirring until gelatin is dissolved. Reserve 1 cup mixture.

Chill remaining gelatin mixture until slightly thickened; fold in strawberries and walnuts.

Meanwhile, to make yogurt layer, gradually beat reserved gelatin mixture into yogurt and nutmeg until smooth. Pour into 4-cup ring mold sprayed with nonstick cooking spray; chill until almost set.

Spoon thickened strawberry mixture over yogurt layer; chill until set. Unmold. Makes 8 servings.

Each serving equals: 1³/₄ Nature's Treats

SIDE DISHES

Hot and Spicy Rice

¹/₄ cup chopped green pepper
¹/₄ cup chopped fresh tomato
2 tablespoons chopped onion
2 medium cloves garlic, minced
4 teaspoons vegetable oil
1²/₃ cups water
²/₃ cup raw regular long-grain rice
¹/₂ teaspoon oregano leaves, crushed
¹/₄ teaspoon cayenne pepper

In medium saucepan, cook green pepper, tomato and onion with garlic in oil until tender-crisp. Add remaining ingredients. Cover; bring to boil. Reduce heat to low; cook 25 minutes or until liquid is absorbed. Stir occasionally. Makes 4 servings (¹/₂ cup each).

Each serving equals: 1 Complex Carb, 1 Palate Pleaser

Creamy Mushroom-Filled Rice Ring

2 cups sliced fresh mushrooms
2 tablespoons finely chopped onion
¹/₂ can (10³/₄-ounce size) condensed cream of
    mushroom soup
¹/₄ cup water
¹/₄ cup skim milk
2 tablespoons Chablis or other dry white wine
¹/₂ teaspoon paprika
¹/₄ teaspoon thyme leaves, crushed
¹/₈ teaspoon pepper
3 cups hot cooked rice (prepared without salt)
1 cup cooked peas
2 tablespoons melted margarine

To make sauce, in saucepan sprayed with nonstick cooking spray, cook mushrooms and onion until tender. Add soup, water, milk, wine, paprika, thyme and pepper. Heat; stir occasionally.

Meanwhile, spray 1-quart ring mold with nonstick cooking spray.

To make rice ring, toss rice and peas with margarine; lightly pack in ring mold. Let stand 2 minutes. Loosen edges; invert on serving plate. Serve with sauce. Makes 4 servings.

Each serving equals: ½ Limited Veggie, 1¾ Complex Carbs, 1½ Palate Pleasers, 1 Flexi-Food

Potatoes au Gratin

½ can (10¾-ounce size) condensed cream of
*   celery soup*
1 cup skim milk
2 ounces shredded reduced-fat process Swiss
*   cheese*
⅛ teaspoon pepper
4 cups thinly sliced potatoes (4 small
*   potatoes)*
1 small onion, thinly sliced
¼ teaspoon paprika
4 teaspoons margarine

To make sauce, combine soup, milk, cheese and pepper. In 1½-quart casserole, arrange alternate layers of potatoes, onion and sauce; sprinkle with paprika. Dot top with margarine.

Cover; bake at 350°F. for 1 hour. Uncover; bake 15 minutes more or until potatoes are done. Makes 4 servings (1 cup each).

Each serving equals: ¼ Dairy Delight, 1 Complex Carb, ½ Protein Provider, 1 Palate Pleaser, 1 Flexi-Food

MAIN DISHES

Pork and Apple Stew

*1 pound boneless pork shoulder, cut in 3/4-inch
    cubes*
4 teaspoons vegetable oil
1/4 cup chopped onion
1/2 can (10 1/2-ounce size) condensed beef broth
2/3 cup unsweetened apple juice
Water
1/2 teaspoon thyme leaves, crushed
1 medium bay leaf
1/8 teaspoon pepper
1 cup sliced carrots
2 small apples, cored and chopped
2 to 3 tablespoons all-purpose flour

Trim fat from pork. In saucepan, brown pork in oil; pour off fat.
Add onion, broth, apple juice, 1/3 cup water and seasonings.
Heat to boiling. Reduce heat to low; cover. Simmer 1 hour 30
minutes; add carrots. Simmer 25 minutes more or until done;
stir occasionally. Add apples.
    Gradually blend 1/4 cup water into flour until smooth;
slowly stir into broth mixture. Cook, stirring until thickened.
Makes 4 servings (3/4 cup each).

Each serving equals: 1 Nature's Treat, 1/4 Complex Carb, 3
                  Protein Providers, 1 Palate Pleaser,
                  1 Flexi-Food

Chicken Chow Mein

1/2 cup diagonally sliced celery
4 teaspoons vegetable oil
1 cup sliced fresh mushrooms
1/4 cup finely chopped green onions
*1/2 can (10 3/4-ounce size) condensed chicken
    broth*

*Pork Apple Stew, Huevos Rancheros, Salmon Cakes
with Mustard Dressing*

³/₄ cup water
2 tablespoons cornstarch
1 teaspoon Worcestershire sauce
¹/₂ teaspoon ground ginger
2 cups cubed cooked chicken
¹/₂ cup bean sprouts

In skillet, cook celery 5 minutes in oil. Add mushrooms and green onions; cook 5 minutes until vegetables are tender-crisp.

In bowl, combine broth, water, cornstarch, Worcestershire and ginger; add to skillet. Cook, stirring until thickened. Add chicken and bean sprouts; heat. Makes 4 servings (³/₄ cup each).

Each serving equals: ¼ Complex Carb, 1 Protein Provider, 1 Palate Pleaser, 1 Flexi-Food

Chicken Divan

1 package (10 ounces) frozen broccoli spears,
  cooked and drained
2 cups cubed cooked chicken
¹/₂ can (10³/₄-ounce size) condensed cream of
  mushroom soup
3 tablespoons Chablis or other dry white wine
¹/₈ teaspoon ground nutmeg
¹/₈ teaspoon pepper
3 tablespoons grated Parmesan cheese

In 1¹/₂-quart shallow baking dish (10x6x2″), arrange broccoli; top with chicken. In small bowl, combine soup, wine, nutmeg and pepper; pour over chicken. Sprinkle with cheese. Bake at 450°F. for 15 minutes or until hot. Makes 4 servings (1 cup each).

Each serving equals: 1¼ Protein Providers, 1 Flexi-Food

Rio Grande Eggplant Casserole

³/₄ pound lean ground beef
¹/₄ cup chopped canned green chilies
¹/₂ can (10³/₄-ounce size) condensed tomato
    soup
¹/₄ cup water
¹/₂ teaspoon ground cumin seed
¹/₄ teaspoon garlic powder
1 medium eggplant, peeled and cut into
    ¹/₄-inch slices
4 ounces shredded reduced-fat process cheese

In large nonstick skillet or skillet sprayed with nonstick cooking spray, brown beef with chilies; stir to separate meat. Pour off fat. Add soup, water, cumin and garlic powder; heat to boiling. Reduce heat to low; cover. Simmer 5 minutes; stir occasionally.

Meanwhile, in separate nonstick skillet, brown eggplant slices, a few at a time. In 1¹/₂-quart shallow baking dish (10x6x2″), arrange 2 alternate layers of eggplant, meat mixture and cheese.

Cover; bake at 350°F. for 30 minutes until eggplant is done. Makes 4 servings.

Each serving equals: 3 Protein Providers, 1 Flexi-Food

Salmon Cakes with Mustard Dressing

1 can (7³/₄ ounces) salmon, drained and flaked
2 eggs, slightly beaten
¹/₂ cup finely crushed unsalted melba toast
    crumbs (12 rectangular pieces)
¹/₄ cup skim milk
1 teaspoon Worcestershire sauce
¹/₈ teaspoon pepper
¹/₂ cup plain lowfat yogurt
¹/₂ teaspoon dry mustard

In bowl, mix salmon, eggs, melba toast crumbs, milk, Worcestershire and pepper; shape into 4 patties. Chill 45 minutes. In skillet sprayed with nonstick cooking spray, brown patties.

Meanwhile, in small bowl, blend yogurt and mustard; let stand 5 minutes. Serve with patties. Makes 4 servings.

Each serving equals: ¼ Dairy Delight, 1 Complex Carb, 1¾ Protein Providers, 2 Palate Pleasers

New Orleans Shrimp Creole

½ cup chopped celery
½ cup chopped green pepper
¼ cup chopped onion
1 medium clove garlic, minced
¼ teaspoon oregano leaves, crushed
4 teaspoons vegetable oil
½ can (10¾-ounce size) condensed tomato
    garden soup
½ cup water
⅛ teaspoon cayenne pepper
¾ pound medium shrimp (about 18), peeled
    and deveined

In saucepan, cook celery, green pepper and onion with garlic and oregano in oil 3 minutes until tender-crisp. Add soup, water and cayenne pepper; bring to boil. Reduce heat to low; cover. Simmer 10 minutes. Add shrimp; simmer 5 minutes more or until done. Makes 4 servings (¾ cup each).

Each serving equals: 1½ Protein Providers, 1 Palate Pleaser, 1 Flexi-Food

Savory Fish Stew

1 medium tomato, cored and chopped
½ cup chopped celery
½ cup chopped green pepper
¼ cup chopped onion
1 medium clove garlic, minced
¼ teaspoon thyme leaves, crushed
⅛ teaspoon pepper
6 tablespoons Chablis or other dry white wine
½ can (10¾-ounce size) condensed
    Manhattan style clam chowder

³/₄ cup water
1 pound fillets of cod, cut into 1-inch pieces

In nonstick saucepan or saucepan sprayed with nonstick cooking spray, cook tomato, celery, green pepper and onion with garlic, thyme and pepper until tender-crisp. Add wine; cook 2 to 3 minutes. Stir occasionally.

Add soup and water; heat to boiling. Add cod; reduce heat to low. Cover; simmer 5 minutes or until done. Stir gently now and then. Makes 4 servings (1 cup each).

Each serving equals: ¼ Complex Carb, 3 Protein Providers, 1 Flexi-Food

Fisherman's Stuffed Fillets

4 ounces canned crabmeat
¹/₂ cup fresh bread crumbs
4 teaspoons melted margarine
1 tablespoon fresh lemon juice
1 tablespoon finely chopped onion
1 tablespoon chopped fresh parsley
¹/₄ teaspoon garlic powder
¹/₈ teaspoon pepper
4 fillets of flounder (1 pound)
¹/₂ cup Chablis or other dry white wine
¹/₂ cup water

To make stuffing, in small bowl, combine crabmeat, bread crumbs, margarine, lemon juice, onion, parsley, garlic powder and pepper. Divide among fillets. Roll up; secure with toothpicks.

In skillet, arrange fillets seam side down. Pour wine and water over fillets; heat to boiling. Reduce heat to low; cover. Simmer 8 minutes or until done. Makes 4 servings.

Each serving equals: 1 Complex Carb, 4 Protein Providers, 1 Palate Pleaser

Giant Cheeseburger

1 1/4 pounds lean ground beef
2 tablespoons chopped onion
1 teaspoon Worcestershire sauce
1/4 teaspoon garlic powder
1/8 teaspoon pepper
8 teaspoons chili sauce
2 slices reduced-fat process cheese, torn into
*   small pieces*

In bowl, mix beef, onion, Worcestershire, garlic powder and pepper. On jelly-roll pan, shape into 7-inch circle; spread with chili sauce. Sprinkle with cheese. Bake at 350°F. for 30 to 40 minutes or until done. Cut in wedges. Makes 4 servings.

Each serving equals: 3/4 Complex Carb, 4 1/4 Protein Providers

Fettucine Bolognese

1/2 pound lean ground beef
1/2 cup sliced fresh mushrooms
1/4 cup chopped onion
1 medium clove garlic, minced
1/2 can (10 3/4-ounce size) condensed tomato
*   soup*
6 tablespoons Burgundy or other dry red wine
1/2 cup cooked peas
1/2 teaspoon basil leaves, crushed
1/8 teaspoon pepper
8 ounces fettucine noodles

In nonstick skillet or skillet sprayed with nonstick cooking spray, brown beef and cook mushrooms and onion with garlic until tender; stir to separate meat. Pour off fat. Add soup, wine, peas, basil and pepper. Heat; stir occasionally.

Meanwhile, cook fettucine in unsalted water following package directions. Toss with soup mixture. Makes 4 servings.

Each serving equals: 1/4 Limited Veggie, 1 1/4 Complex Carbs,
1 1/2 Protein Providers, 1 Flexi-Food

Huevos Rancheros

2 tablespoons vegetable oil
4 corn tortillas (6 inch)
¹/₄ cup chopped green pepper
¹/₄ cup chopped onion
1 medium clove garlic, minced
2 cups chopped fresh tomatoes
2 teaspoons chili powder
¹/₈ teaspoon salt
¹/₈ teaspoon pepper
4 eggs

In skillet over medium heat, in hot vegetable oil, cook tortillas until just pliable; drain on paper towels and keep warm.

In same skillet, cook green pepper and onion with garlic until tender-crisp; add tomatoes, chili powder, salt and pepper. Reduce heat to low; simmer 5 minutes. Stir occasionally.

Meanwhile, in another nonstick skillet or skillet sprayed with nonstick cooking spray, fry eggs until whites are just set.

To serve, top each tortilla with egg; spoon vegetable mixture around egg. Makes 4 servings.

Each serving equals: 1 Complex Carb, 1 Protein Provider, 1¹/₂ Palate Pleasers

Spaghetti with Fresh Vegetable Sauce

1¹/₂ cups chopped fresh tomatoes
¹/₂ cup chopped carrots
¹/₄ cup chopped onion
¹/₄ cup chopped zucchini squash
1 medium clove garlic, minced
4 teaspoons vegetable oil
¹/₄ cup Chablis or other dry white wine
¹/₂ teaspoon oregano leaves, crushed
¹/₂ teaspoon basil leaves, crushed
¹/₄ teaspoon salt
¹/₈ teaspoon pepper
4 ounces spaghetti

To make sauce, in saucepan, cook tomatoes, carrots, onion and zucchini with garlic in oil 5 minutes until tender-crisp. Add wine, oregano, basil, salt and pepper; heat to boiling. Reduce heat to low; cover. Simmer 10 minutes. Stir occasionally.

Meanwhile, cook spaghetti in unsalted water following package directions. Serve fresh vegetable sauce over spaghetti. Makes 4 servings.

Each serving equals: 1¼ Complex Carbs, 1 Palate Pleaser

DESSERTS

Baked Bananas

2 small bananas, cut in half lengthwise
2 tablespoons melted margarine
1 teaspoon ground cinnamon

In 9″ pie plate, arrange bananas. In small bowl, combine margarine and cinnamon; pour over bananas. Bake at 450°F. for 10 mintues or until hot. Makes 4 servings (½ banana per serving).

Each serving equals: 1 Nature's Treat, 1½ Palate Pleasers

Brandied Peaches

4 medium peaches, peeled, halved and pitted
2 teaspoons melted margarine
3 tablespoons brandy
½ teaspoon ground cinnamon

On broiler pan, arrange peach halves cut-side up; brush with margarine. Pour brandy equally in center of each; sprinkle with cinnamon. Broil 4 inches from heat for 5 minutes until hot. Makes 4 servings (2 halves per serving).

Each serving equals: 1 Nature's Treat, ¼ Complex Carb, ½ Palate Pleaser

Tropical Cream Pie

*1 can (8 ounces) crushed pineapple in
    pineapple juice*
2 teaspoons unflavored gelatin
1 cup lowfat cottage cheese
1 cup part-skim ricotta cheese
½ teaspoon coconut extract
½ teaspoon pineapple extract

Drain pineapple, reserving juice. In small saucepan, sprinkle
gelatin over reserved pineapple juice to soften. Place over low
heat, stirring until gelatin is dissolved. In large bowl, combine
cottage cheese, ricotta cheese, coconut and pineapple extracts,
pineapple and gelatin mixture. Spoon into 9" pie plate; chill
until set. Makes 8 servings.

Each serving equals: ¼ Nature's Treat, 1 Protein Provider

Apple Crisp

⅓ cup quick-cooking oats, uncooked
2 tablespoons all-purpose flour
½ teaspoon ground cinnamon
8 teaspoons margarine
2½ cups peeled sliced baking apples (3 small)
1 tablespoon fresh lemon juice

In small bowl, combine oats, flour and cinnamon. Cut in
margarine with pastry blender until crumbly.
    Divide apples among 4 individual (5-ounce size) baking
dishes or arrange in 1-quart casserole. Sprinkle with lemon
juice and oat mixture.
    Bake at 350°F. for 30 minutes until done. Makes 4 serv-
ings.

Each serving equals: ¾ Nature's Treat, ½ Complex Carb, 2
    Palate Pleasers

Raisin and Rice Pudding

4 cups skim milk
1/3 cup raw regular medium-grain rice
2 teaspoons sugar
1 teaspoon vanilla extract
1/2 teaspoon ground cinnamon
1/2 cup raisins

In 1 1/2-quart casserole sprayed with nonstick cooking spray, combine all ingredients except raisins. Bake at 300°F. for 1 hour 30 minutes; stir often. Add raisins; bake 1 to 1 1/2 hours more or until thickened. Makes 4 servings (1 cup each).

Each serving equals: 1 Dairy Delight, 1 Nature's Treat, 1/2 Complex Carb, 1/4 Flexi-Food

KICK-OFF DIET RECIPE FOOD GROUP EQUIVALENTS

RECIPE	EACH SERVING EQUALS:
Fruit Creme	1 Dairy Delight
	1 Nature's Treat
Vegetable Scramble	1 Protein Provider
Herbed Croutons	1/2 Complex Carb
Marvelous Manicotti	1 Complex Carb
	3 Protein Providers
	1 Flexi-Food
Individual Pita Pizzas	1 Complex Carb
	1 Protein Provider
	1 Flexi-Food
Hawaiian Chicken Kabobs	1/2 Nature's Treat
	3 Protein Providers
Curried Cauliflower Polonaise	1/2 Complex Carb
	3/4 Protein Provider
Rice Stuffed Tomatoes	1 Complex Carb
	1 Flexi-Food
Spiced Whole Wheat Pancakes	1 1/4 Complex Carbs
	1/4 Protein Provider
	1 Palate Pleaser
Stuffed Baked Potatoes	1 Complex Carb
Crustless Mixed Vegetable Quiche	1/4 Dairy Delight
	2 Protein Providers
Cucumber Yogurt Dip	1 Dairy Delight
Spicy Green Bean Salad	1 Flexi-Food
Mixed Fruit Sherbet	1 Nature's Treat
Whipped Topping	Freebies
Marinated Vegetable Melange	1 Flexi-Food
Deviled Oven-Fried Chicken	3/4 Complex Carb
	3 Protein Providers
Summer Squash au Gratin	1/4 Complex Carb
	1 Flexi-Food
Frozen Blueberry Yogurt Delight	1/2 Dairy Delight
	1 Nature's Treat

VII

Now It's Your Turn

How often have well-meaning friends and doctors advised you to lose weight, without giving you the slightest idea of how to go about it?

I hope this book has not only motivated you to alter your eating and exercising habits, but has given you concrete direction on how to change them.

You have been given a three-pronged approach consisting of behavior modification, exercise and a sensible, nutritionally balanced diet plan to accomplish your weight-loss and weight-control task.

With behavior modification, we've shown you how to prepare yourself for dieting and how to best assure you lose the weight you want and keep it off. Dr. Foreyt's method of behavior modification, which rewards good behavior rather than punishing you when you slip up, puts you on the road to rooting out ingrained eating habits that can sabotage even the most well-planned diet program.

Kim Stambaugh emphasized the importance of exercise while dieting to reshape and tone muscles and burn extra calories. Losing weight without exercise can leave you with a shape you may not be happy with. And by burning extra calories, exercise makes your dieting task easier.

Developing a regular exercise program can be as important to your weight-control efforts as dieting. The ideal program is one that includes aerobic workouts (to trim inches) as well as lots of stretching exercises (to tone muscles and prevent flabbiness). But in order for exercise to have any positive effect, you should work out at least twice a week, preferably even more. For those who think exercise a chore, "behavior mod" can help get you into the habit of regular exercise, too. Dr. Foreyt says that after 20 weeks of supervised exercise, some people will find the experience so enjoyable that they will continue exercising indefinitely on their own!

The third step in the Soup Diet weight control program is the three eating plans: the Kick-Off Diet, an eating plan consisting of ten days of menus, each day approximately 1000 calories; the Take-It-Off Plan featuring three days of menus at 1200 to 1500 calories; and the Keep-It-Off Forever Plan, with its occasional "Fling Foods," allowing 1700 to 2000 calories for women, 2000 to 2200 for men. All three diet plans conform to the U.S. Dietary Guidelines developed by the USDA and Department of Health and Human Services, recommending reduced amounts of sugar, sodium and fat in our diets. In a later chapter, additional recipes for each diet plan are provided that allow you to choose from approved food groups, rather than simply telling you what you can and cannot have.

The menu plans and recipes are not only well-balanced in the traditional sense, they are also "nutritionally dense." This means that the number of nutrients relative to the number of calories is high, providing you good nutrition for a relatively small number of calories.

You've also seen that soup can help you in your dieting efforts. Many soups are scientifically acknowledged as "nutritionally dense," and because they are served hot, they help us slow down the time it takes to eat a meal. The more slowly we eat, the less we take in.

Finally, you've been shown how to best fit this diet and exercise plan into your daily life. You were given pointers on low-calorie shopping and cooking, and shown strategies for eating out in restaurants and for maintaining your diet while at parties. You were shown how to stay on a diet even if you have to travel.

Dieting can be one of the greatest challenges you face in your life. According to Dr. Foreyt, there are about 80 million Americans with a weight problem. "Weight reduction is one of the most difficult, frustrating problems many of us face in our daily living," he says. "Whether we try drastic measures which are not usually recommended such as the most current fad diet, wired jaws, ear staples, amphetamines, or other more accepted methods such as psychotherapy or hypnosis, most of us simply cannot keep off a large number of pounds."

Weight loss isn't important just for cosmetic reasons, either. Half of the deaths in this country can be attributed to coronary heart disease, which means it outranks even cancer. Chances of developing heart disease can be lessened by controlling certain risk factors, of which two major factors are obesity and lack of exercise. The focus of the Soup Diet is to help eliminate those factors.

The Soup Diet will *help* you in your endeavor to lose weight, not only to look and feel better but to even improve your prospect for good health for many years to come. But in the end, only *you* can do it. So now that you know, there is only one thing to do. Get started!

Bibliography

1. Foreyt, John P., Ph.D. and Goodrick, Ken G., "Weight Disorders" in *Applied Techniques in Behavioral Medicine,* ed. Charles J. Golden, Sandra S. Alcaparros, Fred D. Strider and Benjamin Graber, Grune and Stratton, 1981, pp. 295-319.
2. Kuntzleman, Charles T., Ed.D., *Diet Free,* Rodale Press, Emmaus, Pa., 1981, p. 27.
3. Dusky, Lorraine and Leedy, J. J., M.D., *How To Eat Like a Thin Person,* Simon and Schuster, New York, 1982, p. 30.
4. Stewart, Richard and Davis, Barbara, *Slim Chance in a Fat World,* Research Press, Champaign, Illinois, 1972.
5. Jordan, Henry A., et. al., "The Role of Food Characteristics in Behavioral Change and Weight Loss," *Journal of the American Dietetic Association* 79(1):24-29, July 1981.
6. Schwerin, Horace S., M.A. et. al., "Food eating patterns and health: a reexamination of the Ten-State and HANES I Surveys," *American Journal of Clinical Nutrition* 34:568-580, 1981.
7. Diet Modification Clinic, part of the National Heart and Blood Vessel Research and Demonstration Center at Baylor College of Medicine and The Methodist Hospital, a grant-supported research project of the National Heart, Lung and Blood Institute, National Institutes of Health, Grant No. HL17269. Statements in this book do not necessarily represent policies of the National Heart, Lung and Blood Institute.
8. Select Committee on Nutrition and Human Needs, U.S. Senate, *Dietary Goals for the United States,* 2nd edition, U.S. Government Printing Office, Washington D.C., December 1977.

9. Public Health Service, U.S. Department of Health and Human Services, *Promoting Health/Preventing Disease—Objectives for the Nation,* U.S. Government Printing Office, Washington, D.C., Fall 1980.

10. American Dietetic Association and U.S. Department of Agriculture, *Food 2,* American Dietetic Association, Chicago, 1982.

Index